New Plains Review

FALL 2018

New Plains Student Publishing
University of Central Oklahoma
Edmond, Oklahoma

NEW PLAINS REVIEW is edited by students and faculty of the English Department in the College of Liberal Arts at The University of Central Oklahoma. Political, social, or artistic commentary represents the veiws of the writers and artists, and inclusion in the journal does not indicate editorial endorsement or non-endorsement. New Plains Review does not claim to represent the views of the University or its officials.

The image found on the previous page is from a painting titled *Phantom Warriors* by acclaimed Native American artist and UCO alumnus Sherman Chaddlesone.

Visit our website at *newplainsreview.com*
Email inquiries to *newplainsreview@gmail.com*

English Department, Box 184
University of Central Oklahoma
100 North University Drive
Edmond, Oklahoma 73034

Published in USA; printing & manufacturing information can be found on the final page.

ISBN-10: 0-9984061-3-9
ISBN-13: 978-0-9984061-3-8

Foreword

THE *NEW PLAINS REVIEW STAFF* IS EXCITED TO present the Fall 2018 edition of our literary journal. We would like to thank all of our wonderful contributors for sharing their work with us and with all of our readers. *New Plains Review* is an Oklahoma-based journal, but we accept work from around the world. We are always thrilled with the creative and original work we receive from both our local and international contributors (and all of our contributors in-between). It is our sincere hope that this issue will be a source of inspiration for all who read it.

On behalf of the English Department, College of Liberal Arts, University of Central Oklahoma, we are pleased to present the Fall 2018 edition of *New Plains Review*.

New Plains Review staff

Contents

Our Forever Home

BY ETHAN WARREN

When Nick put the key into the door, it turned so easily that Betsy barely had time to get her phone out. Instead of a photo of Nick ceremoniously opening their new home, she captured his shock as the home seemed to open itself to invite them in—or swallow them up. Betsy couldn't be sure of the apt analogy.

Stepping into the blank hollowness of the kitchen, Betsy was struck by the falseness of her lifelong belief that four walls and a roof provided any real protection. She went to the sliding glass door and looked across the deck at the backyard, considering the three walls of fir trees that kept the untamed forest in check.Nick stepped beside her, and she realized he'd been talking while she drifted away.

"And a swing set," he was saying, "A really nice one. It might have to last long enough for grandkids!"

She spewed a laugh. "Don't get ahead of yourself." She ran a hand over her huge belly and the baby that was so close, yet so distant. "Baby first, grandbabies later."

"But this could be our forever home." He shivered happily and touched her belly. "Don't you feel it?"

She forgot to respond. Those three walls of evergreen gave her the strangest feeling.

They'd only brought a few bags in the car, just enough to survive that first evening, so Nick ordered a pizza while Betsy stepped onto the back deck. The sun was almost down, and as she watched the redness bleed through the branches, she realized just how enveloped they were. If she squinted, she could see the next-door neighbors through the trees, but they wouldn't be passing each other a cup of sugar. Across the street, there were neighbors a few hundred yards in either direction, but looking straight out the front door, there were only more trees. For the first time in her life, she realized it was possible to *hear* silence.

Nick puttered around, monologuing about how to fill the space. There was a trip-step in the middle of the kitchen that put the cooking area three inches above the dining area. Nick hopped up with automatic ease as though he'd lived there for years, while Betsy considered how often their child would stumble, how many bloody lips she'd wipe. The marble counters had such harsh corners, too, at just the height of a careless child's brow. How many other pockets of danger lurked here? She'd been so focused on amorphous fears about leaving the city that she'd forgotten to consider the acute dangers of her new home.

When the pizza arrived, they sat side by side with their backs against the wall, holding their slices on paper towels. Nick mused about the strong rankings of the town's public schools as Betsy forced herself to take a small bite of pizza with all the pleasure of swallowing cardboard.

"I just want us to fit in here, y'know?" He touched her belly, feeling their abstract baby. "Be part of the community." He laughed, and the sound echoed harshly in the empty space. "I got a little kick. What's up, kiddo? You're excited to be part of this place?"

"We don't want a little cog in a wheel, though, right?" Betsy was surprised to hear the rawness in her voice. "Don't we want a unique weirdo?" She attempted a lighthearted smirk to mask her revulsion at the idea that her baby might end up another anonymous denizen of this nameless street, but she couldn't sell it. She forced down another dutiful bite of pizza, and suggested they go to bed early.

Nick's breathing went regular as soon as the lights were out; Betsy wished he'd stay awake and keep her from steeping in loneliness, but she had no interest in talking. Instead, she laid on her side—she couldn't wait to meet this baby they'd dreamed of, and just as much, she couldn't wait to lie on her back again—as she listened to the silence. She could hear the breeze ruffling the needles on the trees.

She must have been awake half an hour—though she would have believed it was ten minutes, or ninety—when the sound started. The high-pitched, grinding squeal was so abrupt that her heart surged painfully, and then she lay still, hyperventilating, waiting for Nick to wake up and go check. But he didn't stir, and she still couldn't fathom talking, so at last she slipped out of the covers and crept downstairs, triggering all the creaking floorboards she hadn't yet learned to anticipate.

The sound was neither louder nor softer downstairs, which seemed strange—even if there were coordinated alarms throughout the house, she should have noticed a change in volume as she moved—so she prowled empty rooms, waiting for the intensity to increase as she neared the source. She knew her fear was reasonable—Was the house filling with gas? Was a system shorting, leaving them moments from conflagration?—but it didn't seem reasonable that the inside of her throat should itch from a trapped scream. This house was a stranger to her, and as she probed it, it felt like a dangerous one worth approaching with caution.

At a loss, she realized the sound could be coming from some device on the exterior, so she forced herself to open the slider, unconsciously closing her eyes. But there was no change in the pitch or volume of that churning whine, even as she stepped out and crossed the deck on bare feet. She could conjure no explanation with a brain that suddenly felt very small in her skull, so she rushed back upstairs, put on headphones, and found the dullest audiobook possible. After an hour or five, she achieved something resembling sleep.

The truck arrived in the morning, and a platoon of men in navy bodysuits removed Nick and Betsy's life and deposited it in the house with ruthless efficiency. As she stood against a wall to watch, Betsy marveled that her sprawling interiority could be so easily condensed, and then with a few slashes of a box cutter spill forth again.

Nick didn't want her to exert herself, he told her he'd do everything and she could just rest, but as he started unloading cookware, she snuck upstairs. She couldn't sit listening to the quiet and wait for the terrible sound to return—though at least that had given her something on which to focus her anxiety.

She unloaded framed pictures from slim boxes, so intent on the work that she didn't hear Nick climb the stairs, and spun around only when he sputtered something about throwing herself into early labor. He wore a face of such naked appall that she wanted to slap it off him.

"I'm barely doing anything!" She bent and removed a picture to demonstrate, but he snatched it. She clenched her teeth to stifle an indignant howl. "I can't just sit around! I'll go crazy!"

"We have to be careful!" He put both hands on her belly; she wished he'd at least go behind her and hug her on his way to worshipping their baby.

He was so palpably sad that she couldn't bring herself to escalate into a fight. "Tell me what I'm allowed to do." He was clearly stung by her wording, but she had no regrets.

"Want to go to the store and stock up a little?"

Her stomach dropped at the idea of venturing into town, as though the house were a space shuttle and leaving would risk rupturing all connection to her life and send her tumbling into freefall. Through a tightening throat, she offered, "What if I go sweep up downstairs?"

That was allowed.

When the sound didn't come that night, its absence disturbed her more than any fear she'd formed in daylight. Had she missed her chance to prevent whatever disaster she'd been warned of?

Without quantifiable trigger, her uneasiness sprawled. Maybe someone was prowling, out in the quiet dark, seeking an unlocked window. There were no neighbors to notice an intruder. She was on her own. For a moment, she tried to reason with herself, then threw off the covers.

She confirmed that the front door, as well as the living room windows, was locked, then peered out onto the front lawn. She didn't see anything, and while that hardly salved her stress, she moved on to check the side door, then went into the kitchen. She remembered the trip-step just in time to save herself from a rolled ankle, grabbing that cold, hard marble corner for support. Stepping down, she checked the latch on the slider, then flipped on the backyard floodlight for one last check.

Three men stood in the precise center of the yard. Her stomach surged so dramatically she thought she might vomit, but she calmed slightly when the men didn't seem notice her—or their sudden illumination.

They wore sharp dinner jackets and bowties, and when they moved, their outfits seemed to gleam, as though there might be some kind of gold lacquer on the fabric. That didn't seem reasonable, but she didn't linger on it. She was busy watching them play croquet.

They each held a mallet, but there was only one ball, and three wickets arranged in a triangle with no stake to be seen. One man—they weren't exactly identical, but they lacked any defining features, and even their ages were impossible to gauge; their bearing seemed simultaneously ancient and spritely—gave the ball a solid thwack, and then all three threw their mallets joyfully to the ground and exchanged warm hugs.

The hugs tipped Betsy from believing they could be neighbors performing some invasive ritual, to realizing they were dangerous lunatics. She ran upstairs, and when she reached the bedroom, she steeled herself to take a peek through the shade before waking Nick.

The backyard was empty. Of course, because it had all been a trick of the eye. She needed rest, she needed to hydrate and eat better. Tomorrow, she'd let Nick feed her grapes and fan her with a palm frond if that was what it took to reassemble reality into something recognizable.

In the morning, the trees were closer. Not by much, but it was irrefutable. She stood at the slider, drinking the small cup of coffee she was permitted, and stared at the space between the deck and the tree line. Most people wouldn't notice, but she'd stared so long at those trees these past few days that she was an expert.

"Don't we get spectacular morning light?" Nick asked as he poured eggs into a pan. "I can't help feeling like this place is our destiny." He shrugged and smiled, and Betsy fought the urge to cover her nose against the pungent egg smell.

After breakfast, he asked if she wanted to go out together for the first big grocery run, but the idea of town gave her the itchy feeling of a transplanted organ struggling to assimilate with its host, so she played the pregnancy card. She waited a few minutes after he drove off, then opened the slider and stepped out.

She stared at the treeline, daring it to dart forward. The trees stared back, so solemnly quiet yet so maniacal. She wondered if they'd start creeping forward as soon as she turned, giggling like mischievous children, or if they were drifting forward now, as imperceptible as tectonic plates. Finally, she trotted down the deck steps, and went to the bulkhead—the spot where the trees were closest to the house—and started counting her steps, precisely aligning her heel and toe. She counted out thirty-two steps, then knelt to use her index finger to measure the additional two knuckles' distance.

She puttered around inside, half-heartedly considering spots to hang art, but she kept a constant eye on the yard in hopes of catching the trees red-handed. She was dimly aware of her absurdity, but the truth of it nagged her so intently that she couldn't ignore it. Finally, when Nick texted to say he was heading home, she gave in and went back outside. She counted the space out once again—and found the trees about a quarter-knuckle closer. Having the truth confirmed rattled her, so she went back and checked again. Same result. In an hour, the forest had come probably an eighth of an inch closer to the house. It was impossible. But it was also true.

She paced in the kitchen, worrying a hangnail. Was it some natural anomaly? Was the house built on some kind of unstable soil? Was that why the realtor had been so eager to unload it? Yes, obviously. She's seen them for the metropolitan morons they were.

She didn't notice her thumb was bleeding until Nick walked in and gasped. She looked down at the red droplets on the floor and tried to wipe them with her socked toe.

"What happened?" he asked, with too much pressure in his voice.

"I don't want to scare you," she said, "but I think we're losing the yard." She knew how she sounded. But she couldn't revise it now, and he was already rushing to the counter.

He grabbed a dish towel and wrapped her hand. "Do you feel OK?"

She nodded, because she couldn't think of anything else to say without sounding crazy.

He opened the towel and looked. "Shit. We need a first aid kit. I'll go back out."

She nodded.

"Would you lie down?"

She nodded again, still not trusting her words, and he lingered long enough that she realized he wanted to see her go upstairs, so she did, and he left, and she snuck back down.

The ache in her mind was the same one that always compelled her to turn back repeatedly and check that a door was locked before leaving town. She put her heel at the bulkhead, and was starting to count paces again when a flash of color caught the corner of her eye. She turned, mouth open to form an excuse, but it wasn't Nick on the deck. It was one of the strange men.

He wore a plaid vest, knee-length pants, and a jaunty cap. He sat cross-legged at the lip of the steps, a serene smile on his face. She went still, some instinct telling her that whatever he might want, it was best not to make the first move.

He stood, dusted his pants, and waved merrily. "Salutations! We must enjoin you to depart this spot."
She'd been halfway prepared to accept him as an eccentric stranger, but now she felt dizzy, like she'd fallen out of the orbit of reality.

"We tender this mere recommendation with utterly magnanimous aims. However, should you and your man elect to remain, you're gonna get gobbled."
She nodded and grunted, all of her energy devoted to parsing his bizarre vocabulary. He trotted down the steps, doffed his cap with a gentlemanly bow, then bounded into the woods.

As soon as he'd disappeared among the evergreens, she ran inside, tears streaming from her eyes before she'd even realized she was on the verge.

◈

When Nick got home, Betsy was standing at the slider, staring hard at the trees. She heard the door open, then a muttered curse, but she didn't turn. She was busy scanning the space between trees for more intruders.

"You said you'd lie down." He grabbed her elbow, gently yet firmly, and she had to force herself not to jerk it away.

She searched for the least alarming way to express herself, landing on, "I don't think we're totally safe here." Not bad. She could work her way to the more upsetting details from there.

He sighed, clearly managing his frustration. "It's natural to feel unsettled. We'll find where we fit in the—"

"I don't *want* to!" She was shocked by her volume and intensity, but it felt right. "I just want to be us!" She rubbed her belly, letting the kid know she was watching out for it, before being struck by an immense wave of lightheadedness.

Nick put a hand on her back, softening in response to her hysteria, which softened her, too. They never could commit to a fight. "I asked the pharmacist for something to help you relax. Something safe for the baby."

Her head swam, so she couldn't offer anything beyond a small nod.

"Do you think you could sleep a little?"

She considered it quickly. If she slept now, then she'd be awake when he slept. Then she could take some serious measurements and make some serious plans.

She let him bring her upstairs.

It was dark when her eyes burst open, and very quiet—even the breeze had died, and Betsy listened in case she could hear the trees move. She must have slept at least ten hours. Now she'd have her wits about her.

She was startled to find Nick in the kitchen, but she'd had so many surprises recently that it hardly rated, so she forced a light laugh and cursed herself for not confirming he was asleep.

"I got hungry!"

"I'll bring you something." His voice was uncomfortably paternal, and she just knew he'd called a doctor and made her an appointment. Suddenly, she did have fight in her, and she was about to unload when she saw them.

"Hey!" She couldn't think fast enough to say anything intelligent, so she went with, "My friends are here!"

Nick followed her gaze and saw the three men stepping out of the trees and into the backyard. "What the hell?"

"It's something that happens here!" It was a relief, at least, that he saw them too.

Wearing their gleaming eveningwear, one man placed the wickets, another dropped the ball, and a third gave it a solid *thwack.*

"Are they neighbors?" He looked at her, accusingly, but she could only shrug as the men dropped their mallets and exchanged those very warm hugs. "I should—" He stopped short because, of course, he didn't know what he should do, so he went to the slider and shoved it open.

"Excuse me!" He leaned out, and Betsy could hear in his voice his obsession with good first impressions.

The men turned to Nick and took stately bows.

Nick was clearly struck by the gentlemanly flourish. "It's

pretty late."

"We did advocate you vacate," one of them said. "You did determine to decline."

Nick threw a shocked look at Betsy, and she shrugged again, because she didn't know either.

"As you elected to linger," the man continued, "you're gonna get gobbled."

The other two nodded.

Nick calmly shut the slider, latching it as he turned to her. "I think we should call the police," he kept his voice calm with what sounded like great effort.

He dialed his cell and listened. "Busy. Do police stations have busy signals?" He was speaking quickly now, and she didn't know if she was meant to respond, which was good, because she couldn't. Nick dialed again, listened, and muttered, "That's weird. Who else should I call?"

Betsy would have liked to speak, but her throat was suddenly very dry. She turned towards the sink, and Nick panicked at the sight of her movement.

"I'll get it!" he yelped, though he couldn't have known what she wanted, but before she could chide him he was rushing towards her. And then his toe caught the trip-step, and his temple caught that harsh marble corner, and he was on the floor.

He was breathing, he wasn't bleeding, but she couldn't rouse him. She slapped him, shouted, pounded on his chest, but he was out, and she was helpless. She grabbed his phone, punched in 9-1-1—busy signal. That seemed so wrong, especially after Nick had gotten the same at the police station, so she tapped open the browser and typed "911 busy signal" in search of some workaround, some shortcut to help. But Nick's data crawled and then died—why hadn't they bothered setting up Wi-Fi yet? Why had they ever decided it was a good idea to live in the goddamn woods where, of course, the data would quit if the wind blew strangely?

She tried 9-1-1 again, her only recourse without access to any emergency numbers. Still busy. And she certainly wasn't dragging her prone slab of a husband out to the car, much less shoving him in. They were stuck.

In the blurred edges of her vision, she noticed the three men climbing onto the deck. One started jiggling the slider—thank God Nick had locked it. As he jiggled, though, the latch loosened, which seemed totally unreasonable, but then the slider was opening, so reason was beside the point.

She sat still, extremely aware of her lack of agility or grace, her lack of any power here, and watched the men remove their jackets, which seemed to glint in the overhead light. She breathed quickly and shallowly, her stomach churning and aching as she waited for them to walk to her and do whatever awfulness they meant to. But they just sat down cross-legged in the middle of the floor in a rough triangle, all facing her.

She waited for them to speak, but after what felt like whole minutes of silence, she couldn't stand it any longer. "Do you know why all the phones are busy and the data doesn't work?"

"That is a component of getting gobbled," one explained.

"And what does that mean?" She heard an awful pleading note in her voice, and her eyes grew hot as she waited for tears to form.

"You opted to linger despite our benevolent contrary advocacy, so now you're gonna get gobbled up."

"Gobbled real good," another man agreed.

"Gobbled right down," said another, or maybe the same one.

She looked out the window in search of any small measure of hope. Instead, she saw the wall of trees had eclipsed at least a third of the yard by now, and the speed seemed to be picking up exponentially. "And the trees moving?"

"Indeed, that's the gobbling."

Their intrusion horrified her and their even keel somehow made it all the worse, adding confusion to the mix. "My husband needs to go to the hospital." Her voice was hoarse, close to a whisper, and she remembered the water she'd wanted before everything went to shit.

The baby stirred in her, waking up and saying hi, and then the tears came. She put a hand on her stomach and felt a small stretch as the little one tried to find a way out into the world, something she now had a sickening suspicion wasn't going to happen.

"Isn't there something I can do to change things?" She took a dramatic sniff, trying and failing to compose herself. She glanced back at the trees. "Is there someone else out there I could talk to?"

She was shocked to find this was what it took to move them. The men leaned towards each other and muttered intently—in school plays, she'd been taught to mutter *peas and carrots* to simulate quiet discussion, and this conference had all the same false and hollow energy. The glimmering on their coats seemed to gather brightness and intensity somehow, but that was probably just her exhaustion and malnutrition. Even the pizza and eggs that had so recently revolted her seemed tantalizing now.

Finally, the men turned to her. "You are approved for colloquy with the concentrate." Then they stood with brisk purpose and left. She heard the front door open and shut, and only then did she wonder what the hell a *concentrate* was.

In the brief silence, it seemed everyone on earth had vanished except herself, this good man that she'd drifted too far from, and this extraordinary baby that she could hardly think about because she couldn't bear the idea that she might not make it to morning—that she might miss seeing the mark it was meant to leave on the world. Outside, the yard had diminished by another six feet at least.

There was a knock at the door. "Come in," she sighed, unable to muster the energy to speak any louder. The door opened, and she heard feet scuffing on the doormat. At least this new invader had manners.

The man who entered wore a tuxedo so dazzling that the only word Betsy could summon was *magnificent*. She couldn't quite identify the color, because when she looked directly at it the brightness hurt her eyes. He had a barrel chest, and must have been at least seven feet tall, so tall that he ducked when he stepped through the kitchen doorway.

"Good evening!" His voice was a baritone as rich as Swiss chocolate, and while he spoke modestly, his words filled the space like a rising tide. "I am the concentrate, and it is a tremendous pleasure to be seen." Betsy was shocked to find some of her terror loosening. Something about this man soothed her, made her sense some glimmer of hope.

The concentrate sat in the middle of the floor, crossed his legs, and clasped his hands.

"Elizabeth, I'd like to play a game."

"My husband needs a doctor." Her voice wasn't meek anymore. She couldn't say how, but the concentrate had brought her to equilibrium.

"Your husband is stable, please trust me. Now let's play a brief guessing game."

Betsy did have a lifelong compulsion to guess a figure and learn how close she was, so she offered her silence, and the concentrate took it as assent.

"How many human beings would you guess have lived on Earth since the advent of Homo sapiens?"

She started trying to organize some figures she could use to extrapolate, but they were too big, so she panicked and blurted, "Twenty billion."

"One hundred and eight billion. Very badly off." He clicked his tongue, disappointed. "Could you guess how many hours of life that adds up to?"

She tried again to begin mental math, but her brain ground to a screeching freeze like an overtaxed computer. "Five hundred trillion?"

"Oh goodness, no. I admit, it's a bit of a trick question. The number of hours lived upon this planet by the species we think of as human is a number so large there isn't a word for it."

She felt scolded, and embarrassed that she'd let herself be distracted. She leveled her sternest glare at him. "All I want to do is leave. If you'd just help me get my husband outside—"

"This one," the concentrate said, leaning forward, snapping her sentence like a twig, "is certainly not a trick. How many hours have you been alive?"

"I don't know!" She was pained by the childish petulance in her voice. "A million!"

"Oh, my word! No, you've been alive a touch over two hundred and forty-nine thousand hours. Your husband, being slightly older, is currently at nearly two hundred sixty-three thousand. Almost half a million between the two of you. You only overestimated your own life by three quarters, not nearly as bad as your guess on the *totality* of human life!" The concentrate laughed with a power that seemed to engulf and crush her, and then sighed. "So, in the grand scheme of things, two people being gobbled is not such a tremendous loss. Can we agree on that? Yes, some people do things that could be called *extraordinary*, but how many in a century? And on a large enough scale, what truly qualifies as significant? Most humans are machines that consume resources and produce nothing." He stabbed the air with a finger. "*But*, if you could instead be a resource? My goodness, that seems like a *tremendously* significant contribution."

The concentrate's features seemed to swim on his face in a way that made Betsy fear she might be on the verge of collapse, so she looked away and saw the trees were only a few yards from the deck now. The concentrate took that moment to stand.

"I just want to go—" She almost whispered *home*, but stopped herself. There was no such place.

"I can make one offer, Elizabeth." The concentrate offered his hand, and she took it, allowing herself to be helped to her feet by his rough, all-encompassing paw. "If you solemnly swear that you will not permit a single selfish thought into your mind, if you think only of the greater good of this sphere into which you happened to be born, then—"

In the millisecond between the concentrate's words, her eyes filled with grateful tears. Time seemed to dilate while she waited for the magic words that would end this test and put things right.

"—the gobbling will be far less painful." He pulled Betsy in for a hug so suffocating she feared the baby would be crushed, and then she was repelled away. Her eyes whirled to the ceiling and she heard the door open and shut.

Then the quiet was back.

She sat very still next to Nick as he started to stir. He touched his head, then jerked his hand back at what must have been a severe tenderness. She only saw it out of the corner of her eye, though. She couldn't look at him. She needed the gobbling to be as painless as possible. For the baby.

"What happened?" Nick pushed himself up to sit next to her.

"We're getting gobbled."

"What's that mean?" She felt his hand grip her knee for support, but to seek comfort by touching him back would be selfish. She couldn't afford that.

"Just focus on how lucky we are."

She felt his head settle on her shoulder. "We really are." She tensed her shoulder to ensure she didn't enjoy these last few minutes with her husband. She had to think of the greater good.

Dead Lock

BY TYLER CORBRIDGE

It's after midnight and the front door is locked. Joe could ring the doorbell, but then what was the point of taking a cab home if he's going to wake Josephine now?

The key should be *here*. Somewhere in his carry-on, if he could just find it….

The outside A/C unit hums, sputters, shakes, rests. Another soft whir from behind—the cab hasn't gone. The driver gives an inquisitive thumbs up, which Joe returns to signal, "I'm good, thanks."

That sound—isn't it the rhythm of someone walking? His wife's bare heels on tile? But no one comes to the door, so Joe knocks lightly, two knuckles, and listens, holding the bouquet of cheap chrysanthemums he purchased from Smell the Roses—a little shop in the airport here in Houston, after landing just an hour ago. They don't look great, a bit wilted, but for what they charge at airports these days….

Dull heels again, moving deeper into the house, into other rooms, onto the deadening carpet. He knocks louder, but she doesn't answer. So he rings the doorbell.

Did Josephine forget her husband flies home tonight? Is he frightening her?

The key is not in Joe's carry-on, nor his suitcase. He goes around back to find the rear entrance locked as well, so he calls his wife's cell. No answer. He calls the home phone. Several faint rings from inside the house, each seeming to follow a longer interval than the last, then the answering machine responds in his own voice:

"Hi, Friend. You have reached Joe and Jo. If you have a message for Joe, press one. If you have a message for Jo, press two. Leave a good one and maybe we'll get back to you."

The recording, which can also be heard playing inside the house, comes through Joe's cell with a delayed effect, resulting in two voices trying to speak over one another.

The A/C gurgles, sputters, and resumes its previous hum as Joe returns to the front of the house. There's the cab, the driver still watching.

After knocking again, Joe thinks he hears his wife speak, but her voice comes muffled through the front door.

"Hunny? What did you say?"

He tries to look in through the window, but the blinds are seamless.

"I brought flowers," he says to the window.

No clear answer. Maybe no answer at all.

A dark animal scutters out of the shadows, crossing his lawn toward the gutter. Then, the faraway sound of footsteps—a man at the end of the street trailing a cigarette, only visible as he inhales, the glowing orange dot fading in and out like a distant lighthouse.

A shadow—what could be his wife—is conjured up by lamplight in the entryway. Is she facing him or is she turned away? *What is she doing with her hands?*

"Jo," he says. Then louder, "Josephine."

She moved, didn't she? The shadow?

"Jo, it's me. Open the—What? Speak up, I can't—"

What is she saying? Anything? Damn the A/C.

"Are you going to make me call another cab?"

Behind him, the cab is still idling. He waits, he listens, and then the amalgamation of the hum and the cicadas and Josephine's soft-traveling voice evokes a memory, or rather a single audible image of his wife sitting expertly erect on a kitchen chair in their backyard, the cello balanced between her knees, dragging her bow deeply.

Joe curses, shakes the doorknob violently, then laughs at the absurdity.

"This is crazy, Jo!" he says.

But he continues listening at the door until his anger subsides. He's becoming pensive, his wife's words still indecipherable but her voice more distinct, not whispering or mumbling. Clear and steady. Her cooly balanced rhythm makes Joe feel as though he's arriving late to some somber conversation they began days ago.

Or years ago. Joe wonders how much he missed while he was away. He wonders how long he's been away. And he wonders, maybe foolishly, over these past eight years, how often have they been speaking to themselves? How many conversations on opposite sides of a deadbolt?

He holds the bouquet to the window and speaks to Josephine through the blinds:

"I brought these all the way from Romania," he says. "From a gypsy girl. So if they're wilted or gloomy, it's only jet lag."

He wants to make her laugh. He wants to be sweet.

"They just traveled a long way to see you is all. They'll be fine in the morning, with some water."

And then—he heard it, didn't he? Thank you? Joe rests the chrysanthemums against the door before taking a step back.

In a minute, he'll rest his head against the cab window en route to a motel. "She wasn't home," he'll say, and he'll close his eyes, trying hard to remember whether or not he removed the tag.

Catarina and Bianca

BY ILZE B. DUARTE

Catarina seemed to hate me from the start. My earliest memories of my older sister involved her telling me what to do, telling me what not to do, and criticizing me. It was relentless. Even her friends bashed me to my face. I figured she had bad-mouthed me to them big time. They all hated me. At school, they shot me contemptuous looks that seemed to say, *here comes Bianca, let's see how we can insult her and make her feel like dirt.*

I didn't understand where Catarina's hate came from. I was shy and withdrawn, your stereotypically awkward pre-teen, and had only a couple of friends—a girl that lived on our street and a girl from school. School was safe. That's where I was happiest. I loved learning and did well in my classes. A few times, I was asked to represent the school in state competitions in language arts and math. I was in student government for two years. A kid in my class told me I "talked difficult." I was generally known as a nerd, although I'm sure back then there was a different word they used for kids who had no life outside of school.

Between school and the time spent with my neighborhood friend, I was able to escape Catarina for most of the day, but eventually I had to go home. And then it would start—her constant meddling, criticizing, name calling. At meal times, with Mom and Dad at the table, she wouldn't dare be rude to me, but she would still find things to argue with me about. We weren't allowed to fight at all, our parents wouldn't have it. That meant that if she started arguing with me, I couldn't talk back. The feelings of distress and anger that Catarina was so good at stirring in me had to stay bottled up inside.

Bianca was everybody's favorite. When you're one of only two siblings, favoritism becomes obvious and even more painful. Bianca could do no wrong. She was the baby, the cute one, the perfect one. Little miss goodie-two-shoes was so irritating! I could see through her. Under that "sweetness" was a selfish girl. When we went shopping for clothes and I showed interest in anything—anything—she'd grab it and go try it on. I don't need to tell you who got to take it home.

She was the bright one, I get it. But I was no dummy

either. I did well in school. But she was always the teacher's pet. One morning, just a few days into seventh grade, the language arts teacher asked the whole class, "Is Bianca's sister here?" I knew who the teacher meant, not only because Bianca isn't a very common Brazilian name (it's Italian), but also because I knew the little twit must have announced, "My older sister has language arts in the next period. Are you teaching seventh grade too?" Just to show everyone how cozy she was with the teacher. I raised my hand. The teacher smiled at me but didn't say anything. I knew she was going to spend the entire year comparing me to Bianca. Oh, lucky me!

The comparisons were endless. Why can't you be well behaved like Bianca? Why don't you wear your hair like Bianca's? Why don't you help around the house like Bianca? I don't remember a single comparison where I ended up at the top. I had much better social skills. I had lots of friends. I got invited to parties. But my mom told me I could only go if Bianca came along. Bianca didn't get along with any of my friends. Without fail, she would start complaining within the first twenty minutes, saying she wanted to go back home. Instead of just enjoying the party, I had to spend most of my time talking the party-pooper into staying longer.

I was good at talking to guys, too. I started dating sometime around sixth grade. When she found out I was seeing someone, she would use it to threaten me. "If you do this or if you do that, I'll tell Mom about your boyfriend!" And she was always around, like a vulture. If a boy was walking me back home from school, she was sure to be just a few feet behind. I had to remind him, "Keep your voice down. Miss tattle-tale is right behind us." Otherwise, whatever we talked about would make it straight to my mom's ears.

Catarina was quite good at lying and seemed to have no compunctions about it. Mom and I suspected Catarina was smoking when we were in high school, but she'd always say she was carrying the cigarettes for a friend. She was always chewing mint gum—to mask the smell of cigarettes in her breath, I thought. The worst, though, was when I found out she was cutting school. In my freshman year in college, I was taking the subway to school when I saw Catarina with her latest boyfriend at the station. She was supposed to be at the college prep course she was taking and our mom was paying for.

I kept my mouth shut, of course. It wasn't my place to tell Mom what Catarina was or was not doing. I was also feeling a bit closer to Catarina at the time and didn't want to ruin it. We were able to go a few days without fighting, and even talked about boyfriends a bit. Or rather, Catarina would talk about boyfriends, and I would listen. I had very little to say from experience, and had mixed feelings about the whole thing. I appreciated the friendly conversations with Catarina, the rare peaceful times, but I wondered if she talked about boyfriends just to rub it in and prove herself superior in that aspect of our lives.

In one of those conversations, Catarina told me that her current boyfriend was married—separated, really, but he was going to get a divorce. So that was why he had never come to the house. Catarina didn't have the guts to bring someone Mom would disapprove of into the house. But she had no qualms about dating the guy, and she had no qualms about telling me about it. Did she have no idea what a burden that would be on me? Was Catarina trying to test me? Or was she merely trying to torture me? It was working. I felt that I was condoning Catarina's actions by keeping her secret, and yet, telling on her wouldn't be right either. It was eating me up inside.

After a few months, Catarina was still seeing the married guy. They didn't go out every weekend, and sometimes they'd go out on a weeknight. Perhaps that's what alerted Mom. One morning, out of the blue, Mom said to me, "There's something fishy about this boyfriend of Catarina's. I wonder if he's married."

I chuckled. Maybe it was the unexpected way that the question had come up. Or maybe it was the awkward way I reacted sometimes to sad or serious news, like the time I had to hide a smile when I was told my friend's father had died. I knew that was a twisted way to react, but there it was. A chuckle. And then I blurted out, "Yes, he is."

Mom's face fell, and I felt responsible for her pain. That was not fair. I wasn't the one who had done something wrong. I wasn't the one who had something to hide. But there was no turning back, the secret was out. I didn't feel pleased or smug or vindicated, just a bit relieved. But I also felt a knot in my stomach. I knew all hell was about to break loose.

I didn't see Catarina until after I came home from my teaching job at night. Catarina looked cross. She glowered at me. "How could you?"

There was no need to ask what she meant.

"Mom caught me by surprise. I blurted it out."

"You could've told her that she should speak to me directly."

"It didn't occur to me," I said.

"It didn't occur to you? I left in the morning thinking everything was okay, only to get back home and have Mom call me a slut, and tell me how ashamed of me she was! Do you think that's fair?"

"You're the one who's dating a married guy. Why am I the villain all of a sudden?"

"It was not *your* secret to tell!"

I wanted so badly for all of that arguing to stop. Catarina seemed to have perfected her ability to wound me with that sharp tongue. My blood boiled, my head felt hot and hazy, and I could not summon the words I needed to stand up for myself. After Catarina reiterated in several ways what a horrible person I was, she stopped talking. I could have felt a few moments of peace then, but I knew there was a lot more turbulence to come.

Catarina didn't stop seeing the married guy. Mom continued to carry the weight of sadness on her shoulders and the lines of disappointment on her face. Catarina continued to glower at me, and the only words she uttered in my direction were of accusation and blame. I had exhausted my responses to her jabs. There'd been no calculation in my telling Mom, because I wasn't the one who had done something that needed hiding. Still, I had to endure Catarina's disparaging remarks day in and day out.

I had felt like a prisoner all my life—from my father's psychological abuse to my sister's hatred and her attempts to control me. My father had already left at that time, but I still had to live with my mom and my sister. In Brazil it's not easy to just pick up and leave. There are no furnished apartments to rent, and if you do find an affordable place to live, it's not customary to room with people you're not related to. That's something I'd only experience later, when I came to the U.S. to study. Back then, I had to stay and endure my sister's vitriol. I was a prisoner in my own home.

Bianca always had it easy. I was the one who had to fight hard for everything—to be allowed to go out with friends, to

have a later curfew, to date someone. At eighteen, I was the one who had to face my dad and ask if he'd talk to my boyfriend. He was nice enough to come to the house and explain to my dad that he had good intentions, asking him if we could date. That's how things were back then. Fathers had all the power. But I had the guts to face my dad and fight for what I wanted. Not Bianca. She was content to free-load off my hard work. A couple of months after my boyfriend sat on the sofa and respectfully asked my dad if we could date, Bianca announced very casually at the dinner table that she was dating someone too. Dad shot her an angry look, but he didn't even lecture. It was that easy for her.

I always had to work harder. When I graduated high school, I took the entrance exam for a bunch of schools. I didn't pass. I had to spend the next year going to prep school in the evenings and working a part-time job during the day. I passed the exam the following year. So did Bianca—on her first try. I would've liked to see her get accepted into an engineering program. I would've made it on my first try too if I'd been trying to get into the frigging letters department!

And then there were the jobs. I applied here, there, and everywhere and would go weeks without hearing back from anybody. Bianca got jobs teaching English in a snap. I had to ask for favors. I would ask aunts and uncles and cousins if they knew someone who worked someplace where there were openings for entry-level jobs.

And then there was the scholarship! A tuition waiver and a teaching assistantship—the red carpet treatment, and a brand-new life handed to her on a silver platter! It just wasn't fair. Bianca was going to hop on a plane and leave, and I was going to stay back and put up with mom's resentment all those months after Bianca betrayed my trust. Did I tell you about that?

In high school, Catarina's dream was to become a chemical engineer. Dad tried to dissuade her, saying it was not a woman's profession. He even brought home a guy, a friend of a friend who worked in the field, to tell my sister what a bad choice that would be. She persevered. She got accepted into a very good chemical engineering program and was doing well, until the labs became more frequent and more intense. It turned out she was allergic to pretty much every chemical she had to handle in her lab classes. She'd come home feeling sick every day. She decided that if she couldn't take the lab a few hours at a time, she certainly wouldn't be able to hold a job where she'd be in the lab all day. So she quit the program. She had to give up on her dream.

I don't know if I could've started over. If I couldn't be an English teacher, what else would I be able to do? I once tried working as a bilingual secretary and hated every minute of it. There was nothing else I liked. If it didn't involve language, I wasn't interested. But Catarina started over. One more time she had to study for the darn entrance exams. She got into a four-year college and majored in business. She started a career in banking, and now she's the local branch manager for a large bank. That's not surprising. She's super smart, so hard-working, and efficient. I guess her bossiness is put to good use in a job like that!

Bianca is a good mother. She's loving but firm with her girls. I hate kids who yell and whine, and I hate parents who do nothing when their kids are behaving badly. Sylvia and Sarah are my princesses, not only because I know I'll never have kids of my own and can dote on those girls to no end, but also because they just are. They're sweet and polite. Don't get me wrong—they're kids. They're mischievous, and they push their limits, but Bianca sets those limits and shows them how to behave properly. I really like that the girls are on a pretty tight schedule too. There's a time to eat, a time to help auntie and grandma pick up the house when they're done playing, a time to take a nap. Kids who do whatever they want, whenever they want, end up exhausted and cranky. Bianca's girls never have the temper tantrums I see so many kids their age get into.

Sylvia's so smart! And she's so pretty. She looks a lot like me. Sarah's smart too, but Sylvia's wise beyond her years. Sarah's the adorable baby, even though she's already starting to walk and talk. She has such a big smile! When they go back home, who's going to brighten up my day?

This visit is going really well. Funny how Catarina doesn't tell me what to do all the time anymore. She still re-makes the bed and re-arranges the toiletries in the bathroom once I'm out of the room, but she keeps mum about it. Maybe she wants to stay on my good side because she loves my girls so much.

Mom still does all the cooking, but Catarina does the dishes. She also does all the shopping for the house. Mom says she's good at finding bargains and getting the most for their money. I'm not surprised at Catarina's knack for money management, but washing the dishes? I'm surprised at her willingness to help out with anything around the house.

Catarina's a very good auntie to my girls. She gives them lots of love and spoils them rotten, but she also respects the rules my husband and I have and actually helps enforce them. Have I earned Catarina's respect? This is so new.

Mom's never been in very good health, but now it's declining so fast. I don't mind all the doctor's appointments and trips to the lab and radiology, but the thing is, she's not getting better. Or rather, one thing gets better, and then another problem starts. And she's not an easy patient. She complains a lot—understandably, I know—but it's hard to get home after a busy day at work and hear all that complaining. It doesn't matter how hard I try or how many specialists I take her to. She's never happy. I think she gave up being happy a long time ago. When Dad left, the abuse stopped, but she never forgave him—again, understandably. But she seems to be proving to the world how unhappy he made her for all those years, by being unhappy for the rest of her life. I know it doesn't make much sense, but that's what it seems like to me. It's so sad to see this. She still has plenty of life ahead of her, but she's given up finding any joy in being alive. And of course she drags me down with her.

Bianca carries merrily on. She knows Mom's not well and calls pretty often. But she lives thousands of miles away. She doesn't see Mom getting worse day after day. She doesn't feel the pain and the burden of caring for someone who doesn't want to get better. Mom's favorite, dutiful daughter isn't here to take care of her. I am.

I'm glad I came home alone this time. Mom's so fragile, so sensitive to noise and movement. She would've loved to see the girls but wouldn't have taken their boisterousness and constant activity well at all.

Mom complained to me that Catarina has no patience with her. Catarina complained to me that Mom's never happy. Catarina whispers, "I don't know how much longer I can take this." She leans slightly on the sideboard, head down, hands flat on the top. I take a step closer and hug her from behind. It must be so hard.

ꕤ

She had to have the surgery. There was no other way.

She was suffering so much. You had to try.

I didn't have to talk her into it. We'd heard of other eighty-year-olds who had heart surgery and survived. We were hopeful.

Of course.

I think I did everything I could.

You absolutely did. You took such great care of Mom.

I do take comfort in that.

It's too bad she couldn't see my girls one more time before she passed.

She saw the video of Sarah singing. She enjoyed it so much. Thank you for sending that.

I'm glad that gave her a little joy.

She was so proud of the girls. And of you too. To her, you could do no wrong.

Really? I sure got my share of disapproval. You know Mom never held back. She'd always tell me when she wasn't pleased with something I did.

I never heard any of that.

Oh, but I did. Recently, actually.

Like what?

How shocked she was when I said Sarah wasn't doing very well in school. As if it were my fault. Or as if I didn't care.

Huh. She didn't mention that to me. Still, she was very proud of you and the girls.

She was proud of you too. She told me several times how devoted you were to her. I hope you'll take good care of yourself now.

What do you mean?

Get out more, start dating again.

Oh, believe me, I will. But right now I need some downtime.

Can I help with anything? What're you going to do with her room?

Nothing right now. I can't touch anything.

Too painful, huh?

It's not just that. I believe she's still here in spirit and may not even know she's passed. We need to be respectful of her space for a while. I know you don't believe in that kind of thing.

Well, I feel her presence all around. That's for sure.

Arrival Day

BY RACHEL BROWNING

"Sean, why does the couch smell like beef jerky?" Melanie calls from the living room. I'm in the kitchen scouting for cleaning supplies, but I can picture my wife's scrunched brow. I hesitate before answering.

"I mistook the can of mesquite grill spray for upholstery cleaner," I say. "Sprayed the cushions. Accidentally, I mean."

"What? How is that even *possible*?"

"The cans. Same color. Don't worry, I'll clean it."

"And how do you plan to do that?"

"Soap and water. A sponge." I meet her in the living room to accept my punishment.

Hands planted on her hips, she shoots me a look and mulls over the damage. "That won't work. I'll have to remove the covers and put them in the wash."

"Sorry, Mel; just trying to be proactive."

It's the longest conversation we've had in about a week. After receiving the call from our adoption caseworker four days ago, though, Melanie shifted into high gear—rescheduling her piano students, stuffing the freezer with casseroles, phoning relatives. She's apparently even made time in the day's schedule for my screw-ups.

"Have you finished putting together the crib?" she asks.

Shit. The crib. Yesterday, I'd unpacked all the components onto the nursery floor and examined the dizzying instructions while our five-year-old son Caleb stood next to me, armed with his toy hammer. After a half-hour, we'd abandoned the project and gone to Dairy Queen for Blizzards. I start to remind her that we won't need the crib for a while. I know she's going to want to keep the baby in the bassinet in our room. Last time we hadn't bothered to get a crib beforehand. But I can see Melanie wants to do things differently this time.

"Yep. The crib. That's where I'm headed next," I say.

Melanie rolls her eyes, removes the cushions from the couch, and unzips the oily covers like she's skinning a dead animal. As she marches them to the laundry room, I follow, knowing she'd prefer to confine the topic of discussion to this task. But I'm tired of holding my breath.

"Look, honey; I know I should've been more forthcoming," I begin.

"Sean, let's not do this now. Let's really, fucking not."

"Mel, listen to me. We're about to become parents. Again. Finally. We should talk about this. Before everything gets too crazy. I just need you to understand."

She shoves the covers into the washing machine, adds some detergent, and slams the lid—like I haven't already figured out that she's pissed. "What I understand is that you and your editor want to *exploit* our trauma," she says.

"Wait. Don't you think that's a little extreme?" I ask, and immediately regret it.

"No, I do not. And don't try to minimize this."

"I'm not minimizing anything."

"Admit it: you're more comfortable sharing your pain with the public than with me. I mean, really, a *memoir*? If I hadn't overheard you on the phone…"

"I was going to discuss all of it with you. Eventually," I say. "Maybe you can contribute to the book. It could be a collaboration."

She closes her eyes and exhales like she's about to start meditating. "Look. I can't deal with this right now. Would you please just go finish the crib? We have to leave in three hours."

"Fine. But there will be follow-up visits from the caseworker. I think the agency prefers for adoptive couples to at least be on speaking terms." I head for the stairs. "I'll have the crib done in thirty minutes. Then we are having this conversation."

Melanie knows I'll be lucky if I can identify the correct hardware in thirty minutes. I'm not a *build-it* kind of guy. Or a *fix-it* guy. I'm a musicology professor at the University of Washington—a specialist in late-Romantic classical music, particularly the music of Gustav Mahler, the inspiration for the biography/memoir I'm writing. Or trying to write. I have a photographic memory and an ear that can recall every score I've ever studied. I can read, write, and speak three languages. But if the garbage disposal so much as chokes on a sweet potato peel, we phone the plumber. I've never even changed a flat tire.

Melanie knows all this. The crib project is just a way to get me out of her hair while she renovates the entire house before going to meet our baby.

She knows the origins of my quirks and obsessions because, ten years ago, she was my student. I was a Ph.D. candidate and teaching assistant at Indiana University, where she was working on her master's in piano performance. She was required to take my seminar on Mahler to satisfy the music history portion of her degree.

She stood out the very first day of class, leaning back in her seat, legs crossed, hair the color of caramel gathering at her shoulders, her dark, penetrating eyes studying me. Initially, her fierce attention caught me off-guard. Most performance majors slumped over their desks glassy-eyed, barely conscious. Melanie was different. Throughout the term, she asked questions of depth and substance, twirling her pen between her long fingers as she considered my responses. Sometimes I wondered if she was just trying to stump me.

I lectured on, occasionally returning her gaze with unveiled curiosity, trying not to imagine the taste of her lips or the sweep of her hair against my bare chest. I began to believe that she was the only person listening, that we were the only two people in the classroom, that it would only ever be the two of us in any room, anywhere.

Just before the start of the second semester, I was having a bourbon at a sports bar a few blocks from campus while pretending to watch a Knicks/Pacers game. A January gale had whipped up towering drifts of snow, clogging Bloomington's already narrow streets, postponing classes. Melanie appeared out of nowhere and pulled up a stool next to mine. She unwound her scarf and ordered a Black and Tan, a perennial fixture on the happy hour menu that I didn't know people actually drank.

"So, I'm guessing Mahler was a terrible lover," she said. I nearly snorted my drink.

"Uh…Thanks for sharing. I guess," I stammered. I looked over each shoulder to see if anyone was with her. "Did you know I would be here?" I asked.

"Think about it: he worked and traveled constantly, had a weak heart, and was obsessed with his own mortality." she continued, "His wife must've been miserable." When the bartender slid her drink over to her, she dipped her finger into the foam and lifted a dollop to her lips.

"You make an interesting point," I said, uncertain if I should take her remarks seriously or attempt to respond with something that might charitably pass for humor. "But… He got Alma pregnant before they were even married. She had reasons to be miserable, but the sex with Gustav probably wasn't one of them."

She regarded me with amused skepticism.

"In any event, the class is over," I added. "You can stop trying to impress me."

Her eyes widened as she took a long swig of beer. I considered going outside and throwing myself into the path of an oncoming snowplow. I'd always sucked at flirting. But when I returned to my drink, she slid her hand over and rested it on my inner thigh. I met her gaze and laced her chilled fingers in mine.

"I could say the same thing to you," she said.

"Just finish your drink," I said.

By midnight we were disentangling ourselves under lambs-wool blankets on her living room rug—our bodies spent, yet awakened. She asked me to stay the night. I remained for a whole week while winter gathered outside and the stacks of study materials for my upcoming oral examinations collected dust in my apartment.

During the next year, we were inseparable, spending most of our time at her place, where I graded papers and memorized flash cards to the soundtrack of her daily regimen of Bach, Schumann, and Chopin. She was willing to listen to me blather on about my dissertation on the theoretical and programmatic evolution of Mahler's symphonic song cycles, sometimes editing what I'd already written. Occasionally, we would talk about the future—we were both in our early thirties, so it seemed like the right thing to do. All I knew was that I wanted her. I wanted this feeling we'd captured to envelop and carry us wherever we went. I assumed that everything else we would need for a fulfilling life together would follow.

Today, in less than three hours, we'll meet our infant daughter. That's what's supposed to happen, anyway. I know Melanie's trying not to anticipate the worst. I know because that's what I'm doing. I'm trying not to recall that it was five years, three months, and ten days ago that Melanie's failed delivery brought us Caleb but took his twin sister Evelyn in return. Or two and a half years since the second miscarriage. Or just one year since receiving the news from our adoption agency, on the way to the hospital, that the birth mother had decided to keep her child.

I'm trying to shed that cloak of longing that has shrouded us these last five years, the belief that the family we never knew we wanted would always be just out of reach. Maybe I've learned to absorb the disappointment—like skin adapting to the initial abrasion of wool. But now I want it discarded. So, I'm telling myself that this time will be different. We're bringing Caleb's sister home today.

In the nursery, the numerous crib parts line the floor, labeled with capital letters that, yesterday, Caleb had proudly arranged alphabetically. He's not here to help now—he's at a friend's for a playdate so that we can prepare for the baby's arrival in peace. We plan to pick Caleb up on our way to the agency.

I grab the screwdriver and Allen wrench from my toolkit and revisit the instructions, hoping it won't be as overwhelming as I'd feared.

After a half-hour, I'm still at it. It's tedious, my body aches from the crouched positions it's requiring me to endure, and I can barely feel my fingers.

"How's it going?" Melanie appears in the doorway holding a basket of towels.

"Making progress," I say. "Just trying to attach the mattress support—damn, that doesn't work." The holes aren't lined up right, and one of the rails slides to the floor with a sharp thud. Melanie sets the basket down and takes a seat next to me.

"Let me help," she says. "I need something else to do." She's put on makeup, but her eyes still reveal that she hasn't slept in days. Neither of us has.

"Then, here. Hold this," I say, and Melanie takes the side rail from me and balances it in place while I reattach the tabs for the mattress support. This time, they click into place.

When it's finally finished, we study our joint accomplishment in silence, then lift the crib over to the corner of the nursery. A mobile of pastel-colored safari animals dangles above it—the only other fixture in the pale grey, sunlit room. I'd waited until yesterday before ordering the changing table, bureau, and rocking chair, figuring that, if things don't work out again, I can cancel the order before it ships. Maybe I should've told Melanie that, too.caught me off-guard. Most performance majors slumped over their desks glassy-eyed, barely conscious. Melanie was different. Throughout the term, she asked questions of depth and substance, twirling her pen between her long fingers as she considered my responses. Sometimes I wondered if she was just trying to stump me.

I lectured on, occasionally returning her gaze with unveiled curiosity, trying not to imagine the taste of her lips or the sweep of her hair against my bare chest. I began to believe that she was the only person listening, that we were the only two people in the classroom, that it would only ever be the two of us in any room, anywhere.

Just before the start of the second semester, I was having a bourbon at a sports bar a few blocks from campus while pretending to watch a Knicks/Pacers game. A January gale had whipped up towering drifts of snow, clogging Bloomington's already narrow streets, postponing classes. Melanie appeared out of nowhere and pulled up a stool next to mine. She unwound her scarf and ordered a Black and Tan, a perennial fixture on the happy hour menu that I didn't know people actually drank.

"So, I'm guessing Mahler was a terrible lover," she said. I nearly snorted my drink.

"Uh…Thanks for sharing. I guess," I stammered. I looked over each shoulder to see if anyone was with her. "Did you know I would be here?" I asked.

"Think about it: he worked and traveled constantly, had a weak heart, and was obsessed with his own mortality." she continued, "His wife must've been miserable." When the bartender slid her drink over to her, she dipped her finger into the foam and lifted a dollop to her lips.

"You make an interesting point," I said, uncertain if I should take her remarks seriously or attempt to respond with something that might charitably pass for humor. "But… He got Alma pregnant before they were even married. She had reasons to be miserable, but the sex with Gustav probably wasn't one of them."

She regarded me with amused skepticism.

"In any event, the class is over," I added. "You can stop trying to impress me."

Her eyes widened as she took a long swig of beer. I considered going outside and throwing myself into the path of an oncoming snowplow. I'd always sucked at flirting. But when I returned to my drink, she slid her hand over and rested it on my inner thigh. I met her gaze and laced her chilled fingers in mine. "I could say the same thing to you," she said.

"Just finish your drink," I said.

By midnight we were disentangling ourselves under lambs-wool blankets on her living room rug—our bodies spent, yet awakened. She asked me to stay the night. I remained for a whole week while winter gathered outside and the stacks of study materials for my upcoming oral examinations collected dust in my apartment.

During the next year, we were inseparable, spending most of our time at her place, where I graded papers and memorized flash cards to the soundtrack of her daily regimen of Bach, Schumann, and Chopin. She was willing to listen to me blather on about my dissertation on the theoretical and programmatic evolution of Mahler's symphonic song cycles, sometimes editing what I'd already written. Occasionally, we would talk about the future—we were both in our early thirties, so it seemed like the right thing to do. All I knew was that I wanted her. I wanted this feeling we'd captured to envelop and carry us wherever we went. I assumed that everything else we would need for a fulfilling life together would follow.

Today, in less than three hours, we'll meet our infant daughter. That's what's supposed to happen, anyway. I know Melanie's trying not to anticipate the worst. I know because that's what I'm doing. I'm trying not to recall that it was five years, three months, and ten days ago that Melanie's failed delivery brought us Caleb but took his twin sister Evelyn in return. Or two and a half years since the second miscarriage. Or just one year since receiving the news from our adoption agency, on the way to the hospital, that the birth mother had decided to keep her child.

I'm trying to shed that cloak of longing that has shrouded us these last five years, the belief that the family we never knew we wanted would always be just out of reach. Maybe I've learned to absorb the disappointment—like skin adapting to the initial abrasion of wool. But now I want it discarded. So, I'm telling myself that this time will be different. We're bringing Caleb's sister home today.

In the nursery, the numerous crib parts line the floor, labeled with capital letters that, yesterday, Caleb had proudly arranged alphabetically. He's not here to help now—he's at a friend's for a playdate so that we can prepare for the baby's arrival in peace. We plan to pick Caleb up on our way to the agency. I grab the screwdriver and Allen wrench from my toolkit and revisit the instructions, hoping it won't be as overwhelming as I'd feared.

After a half-hour, I'm still at it. It's tedious, my body aches from the crouched positions it's requiring me to endure, and

I can barely feel my fingers.

"How's it going?" Melanie appears in the doorway holding a basket of towels.

"Making progress," I say. "Just trying to attach the mattress support—damn, that doesn't work." The holes aren't lined up right, and one of the rails slides to the floor with a sharp thud. Melanie sets the basket down and takes a seat next to me.

"Let me help," she says. "I need something else to do." She's put on makeup, but her eyes still reveal that she hasn't slept in days. Neither of us has.

"Then, here. Hold this," I say, and Melanie takes the side rail from me and balances it in place while I reattach the tabs for the mattress support. This time, they click into place.

When it's finally finished, we study our joint accomplishment in silence, then lift the crib over to the corner of the nursery. A mobile of pastel-colored safari animals dangles above it—the only other fixture in the pale grey, sunlit room. I'd waited until yesterday before ordering the changing table, bureau, and rocking chair, figuring that, if things don't work out again, I can cancel the order before it ships. Maybe I should've told Melanie that, too.

"We still make a good team," I say, trying to navigate us back to neutral territory.

"You think?" she asks, but then turns to leave. "I should see if the cushion covers are done."

I know our paths of coping with the relentless uncertainty diverged long ago, but I can no longer pinpoint when.

"It's been my way of processing everything," I say. "The book, I mean."

"God. This again?" She picks up the basket of towels and heads for the stairs.

"Wait, Melanie," I say, and I'm surprised when she turns back to face me. "I started keeping a journal, sort of, after what happened, you know, to Evelyn. I should've told you then; I get that. Maybe it's a guy thing. Or maybe I just needed to keep something for myself. We were all going through so much."

"I don't mind your keeping a journal, Sean," she said, annoyed. "What I mind is…"

"After a while, it became something more. I started thinking about Mahler differently. This man, the source of my career, he began to feel … more real, more human. Like family. And so, I knew I couldn't just write another biography about some mercurial, long-dead composer. I saw a unique opportunity."

"What the hell are you talking about?" She lets the basket drop to the floor.

"Come on, Melanie. Don't you see?"

She stares at me, utterly baffled, and I can feel the sweat forming on my brow. I'm back in graduate school, offering a floundering defense of my dissertation.

"He and Alma lost a child; we lost a child…" I explain.

"Mahler was obsessed with death; you're obsessed with death," she adds.

"No, that's the thing, that's the difference. I'm not. And that's what I want to write about—how we managed to keep going. I'm not explaining it right. Look, I had to do something with the pain, okay? Work with it, create something from it. I couldn't just sit around and…"

"And what? Wallow? Like I did?" Her eyes search mine through a haze of weariness and frustration.

"No, I don't think that's what you did. I know it was different for you," I say. *I've been here for you this whole time,* I want to add, but Melanie's out the door and on her way down the stairs before I get the words out. We're two hours away from leaving and back in a stalemate.

⚘

After we lost Evelyn, the simplest tasks felt intolerable. Melanie's body, depleted from the delivery and subsequent surgeries, had nothing left to give. Caleb needed her nonetheless. The doctors agreed that giving him formula was acceptable under the circumstances. I handled the midnight feedings while Melanie tried to sleep.

Then we watched, bleary-eyed, as Caleb grew and toddled and ran, moving and diving as fast and as far from us as his stocky legs could carry him, the shriek of his laughter trailing behind. We tried to keep up with him and celebrate this miraculous, growing boy, even as each birthday and milestone he reached brought another reminder of who we'd lost.

The cleaning began after Melanie's miscarriage three years later. Within hours of returning from the doctor, she had donned yellow rubber gloves and had battened her hair down with a scarf. She canceled her students' lessons. "Do you have any idea the germs they're bringing in here?" she'd asked when I suggested she needed to rest. For a week, she washed, dried, and pressed the curtains, dusted between the slats of the blinds, steam-cleaned the rugs, scoured and polished every crevice of the house, while The White Stripes growled from the living room stereo. I wondered if she wasn't onto something—maybe the universe wouldn't allow us another child until we'd thoroughly disinfected our repellent home.

But a year ago, after the failed adoption, there was no cleaning on her part. Or doing much of anything. For days, Melanie remained in our room alone; blinds closed, television muted, unread magazines strewn across the bed. I tried to persuade her to get up, take a bath, take a walk. I thought maybe we needed counseling. "It won't change things," she said. I brought her orange slices and green tea, the only things she would agree to eat or drink. "I can't think—my mind is a tub of wet cement," she said, and I imagined the slow-churning matter oozing into her every nerve and capillary, hardening her into an immovable effigy of grief.

We needed to get away—from the house, the nursery, the boxes of baby gifts still piling up in the dining room. Orcas Island wasn't too far—The San Juan's were where we'd spent our honeymoon. "Whatever; it's fine," Melanie said, appearing to lack even the energy to object. I told her she wouldn't have to leave the cabin if she didn't feel like it.

The car crammed with our suitcases, food, Caleb's books and games, and my research materials, we made the three-hour trek up the interstate from Seattle to Anacortes. From there, a ferry guided us over water that gleamed like marble, around island hills blanketed in fir and cedar. Caleb staked out a position at the front of the top deck. Like a captain at the helm of a ship, he monitored the ferry's trajectory, while I pointed out the names of the islands dotting his map—Decatur, Lopez, Shaw, Orcas. Impatient, he kept asking where all the whales were. "They don't hang out here, Buddy," I told him. "Too much traffic."

Melanie remained inside the ferry at the café. I was just glad she'd left the car.

For the first five days of the trip, she kept to our cabin. While Caleb and I hiked and kayaked and befriended a local fisherman who showed Caleb how to bait a hook and cast a line, she slept in and watched HGTV, while flipping through the cabin's endless supply of *People* magazines. At night, she ate whatever we cooked, sipped pinot noir, and half-listened as Caleb, blue eyes beaming, recapped the day's adventures, one story zigzagging into the next.

On the morning of the sixth day, however, I awoke just after sunrise to find Melanie already up, sitting in the rocker on the porch, a freshly-brewed cup of coffee cradled in her hands. On the table next to her was a stack of brochures and a copy of the local paper.

"You're up early," I said. "What a great morning." The air was damp, and a light breeze shuffled the leaves and swept us with the scent of balsam.

"We should go on a whale watch," she said, handing me one of the brochures. "We don't need a reservation. We can just show up." She took a sip of her coffee. A glint of self-satisfaction stole across her face.

"Okay," I said. "Let's do it."

A few hours later, Melanie was fastening Caleb into a life-vest aboard a powerboat while our guide explained the day's route and what we could expect to see. The skipper eased the boat away from shore and into the strait. As we sped off through the smooth water, a train of white foam formed behind us, the wind whipping at our eyes and through our teeth. Soon, the dock, marina, and entire island were invisible, and all that surrounded us were collections of other tiny islands, seemingly uninhabited. I felt like I could breathe again.

After about forty-five minutes, we encountered a gang of harbor seals, a couple of ospreys, and other seabirds, but no whales.

"Where are they?" Caleb asked for about the tenth time as the boat gradually came to a rest and rocked in the choppy water.

"It's not like at SeaWorld, kiddo," I explained. "The whales aren't exactly waiting for us. They like to travel with their families, and it might take a while to find them."

Melanie had been quiet for the duration of the trip, occasionally snapping pictures with her phone or peering through a pair of binoculars. So, it surprised me when she suddenly pointed and said, "There, Caleb. Look!" as several curved black figures appeared in the water about two-hundred feet from the boat.

"Where? Lemme see, lemme see," Caleb exclaimed. Melanie lifted him in front of her and fitted the binoculars over his eyes.

We watched as the whales glided and dove and reemerged, cresting just above the surface of the water, over and over and over—the four of them in graceful unison. Occasionally, one of them would lunge, or breach, revealing its chalk-white chest and sides. I took more photos, at Caleb's insistence. But mostly, I just watched, not only the whales but also Melanie with Caleb, wiping his windswept curls from his eyes, adjusting the binoculars, smiling, taking it all in.

⚜

I head back downstairs and find Melanie at our kitchen island staring at the diaper bag. Several tiny diapers, a package of wipes, some burping towels, and three little bottles of formula sit next to it. The agency told us we'd need to be there a while to complete some additional paperwork.

"You got up," I say. Melanie doesn't look at me. "You didn't *wallow*," I continue. "You got up. You left your bed; you left the cabin. It was you who put us back on the waiting list. And now, here we are. We survive, no matter what. That's what I want people to know."

"I don't know." She looks down and positions then rearranges the items in the bag.

"Well, okay. So… Let's talk later and figure out what…"

"I don't know if I can do this, Sean," she says, her voice just above a whisper.

"What do you mean? Do what?"

"*This*," she says, gesturing to the bag. "Be a good mother to this child. After everything." She zips the diaper bag shut and hugs it to her chest.

I'm at a loss for how to respond. I think about the turmoil of the last five years. What I should have said when, what I could have done differently. My mind is a jumble of hopes, doubts, regrets.

I move behind her and place my hands on her shoulders. "I'm scared, too," I say.

Melanie lets go of the bag and leans back, and I feel her body relax against mine. We stay like that for the next several minutes, breathing in unison, absorbing the passing stillness of the room and the dawning recognition that the rest of our lives is finally about to begin.

Exit Strategies

BY ANDREW R. HEINZE

Genre: Comedy

Run Time: 10 mins.

Brief Synopsis: CHRIS, a writer, makes a last desperate phone call to a company that caters to the suicidal. The call is taken by JORDAN, a sales rep who delivers much more than the product CHRIS had intended to buy.

Characters: CHRIS (m or f; 30s); JORDAN (m or f; 30s)

Script Format: Dramatists Guild

Time: The present.

Place:A city apartment and a call center.

JORDAN sits by a phone in a call center. CHRIS is at a fourth-wall window, leans out, looks down to the street far below, gets anxious, phones.

JORDAN

Exit Strategies, Writer's Department, this is Jordan, how may I help you?

CHRIS

Is this the Writer's Department?

JORDAN

Writer's Department, this is Jordan, may I help you?

CHRIS

Sorry I repeated that. It's just … I wasn't sure if I dialed the right extension.

JORDAN

This is Jordan, may I help you?

CHRIS

Yes, Jordan, OK, hello—

JORDAN

—To whom do I have the pleasure of speaking?

CHRIS

Oh. I'm—my name is—uh…

JORDAN

To whom do I have the pleasure of speaking?

CHRIS

Do your customers use their real names?

JORDAN

Oh yes. By the time they come to us, they don't care anymore. To whom do I have the pleasure of speaking?

CHRIS

OK. My name is Chris.

JORDAN

Hello, Chris. How are you doing today?

CHRIS

How am I—oh, well, since I'm calling you, I guess not so well. How are you?

JORDAN

Comme ci comme ça. How may I help you?

CHRIS

OK. Yes. I've checked out your site, but I want to make sure I understand exactly what I'll be getting if I decide to purchase.

JORDAN

OK, sure. Before we discuss those options, I need to inform you that we are on a recorded line and that Exit Strategies does not endorse, recommend, or encourage any actions that conflict with federal law, state law, or the happiness and peace of mind of our customers. Would you like to continue?

CHRIS

Yes.

JORDAN

OK, so products. We offer the Plath, the Hemingway, the—

CHRIS

—Sorry to interrupt, but before I choose a specific item, I want to know exactly what you'll provide. I understand there are two parts, the info packet and the writing sample, correct?

JORDAN

"Info packet" hardly describes what you'll receive. Yes, we provide information about the method used by the author you've selected, but that would hardly be a service worth paying for, would it?

CHRIS

I guess n—

JORDAN

—Seriously. You could google that, couldn't you?

CHRIS

Yes, I—

JORDAN

—What we provide, what is worth your hard-earned dollar, what cannot be found in a mere web search, is our explanation of the side effects of each method.

CHRIS

Side effects?

JORDAN

For example, by the time our customers call in, they've already contemplated a preferred method. Shall we start there? What's yours?

CHRIS

I wasn't prepared to get into that level of—

JORDAN

—Shall we start there? What's yours?

CHRIS

Jumping out the window.

JORDAN

Ah. Self-defenestration.

CHRIS

Ok, yes. I almost did before I called you.

JORDAN

Well thank God you didn't. Didn't you wonder why we offer no self-defenestration product?

CHRIS

No, I—

JORDAN

—Exit Strategies is not just about methods, we're also about impact. No pun intended. Our mission? To fully inform our customers about the unforeseen consequences of what they're about to do.

CHRIS

What kind of unforeseen consequences?

JORDAN

Well, you'd have to purchase the product, wouldn't you? I mean, it's part of what we offer. If we give it away, we're not really a business, are we?

CHRIS

No. Of course. I wasn't trying to get something for nothing.

JORDAN

I know you weren't. I'll give you one little bit of the answer. You could hurt someone. Probably kill them.

CHRIS

I would look down first. Obviously. Give me some credit.

JORDAN

Sure, you look before you leap, but what if someone happens to emerge after you leap? Maybe from a hidden doorway? Or they're running to catch a bus? Too late for them. And now that you realize that what you call the "Info Packet" is much more than that, let's move on to the second component of our service, the writing sample. This is simple. We take the written material you submit and refashion it in the style of the author you've chosen. The result? A goodbye note of outstanding literary merit.

CHRIS

Can the customer—

JORDAN

—Comment on the text? Of course. You're entitled to review our work and make any changes you desire. Realizing, of course, that the revised text we send you has been rigorously styled by a staff of top-tier writers. We hire only MFAs, Ph.D.s, and authors with at least three publications in peer-reviewed journals of literary fiction. Questions?

CHRIS

No, I think I—

JORDAN

—OK, so products we offer are the Plath, the Hemingway, the Mishima, the—

CHRIS

—What's the Mishima?

JORDAN

As in Yukio Mishima? Who committed seppuku? You know, disembowel—

CHRIS

—I know what seppuku is. Do a lot of people go for that?

JORDAN

It's a niche market, not one of our big box products so to speak. Actually we had a controversy over the Mishima last year.

CHRIS

Controversy?

JORDAN

Someone accused us of cultural appropriation. We explained that stabbing yourself in the gut was as American as apple pie, but they tried to counter that it isn't the stabbing, it's the method of turning the—

CHRIS

—I don't need the details. It's not my kind of thing.

JORDAN

So we have the Plath, the Hemingway, the Mishima, the Woolf, the—

CHRIS

—Wait. The Woolf?

JORDAN

Yes, the Woolf, as in Virginia—

CHRIS

—I know which Woolf. What I'm asking is, do people actually do themselves in by stuffing their pockets with rocks and walking into a river? I mean, I thought that was unique to her.

JORDAN

You'd be surprised. So where was I? The—

CHRIS

—Are you getting this stuff off a prompt sheet or are you a big reader?

JORDAN

Stuff? What do you mean, stuff? These kernels of biography? Of history's greatest authors? Tortured souls overwhelmed by the burden of existence? You call that "stuff"?

CHRIS

I meant no offense. I just suddenly realized how depressing it would be if I was having this conversation with someone who had no idea who these people were.

JORDAN

If I'm not mistaken, you have reached the Writer's Department. Would you like me to transfer you to another—

CHRIS

—No, I didn't mean to offend you, I only wanted to know if—

JORDAN

I can read at a sixth-grade level?

CHRIS

No! I—

JORDAN

—Wanted to be sure Exit Strategies personnel have completed their G.E.D.?

CHRIS

No! Only if—

JORDAN

—I'm a writer?

CHRIS

Are you? A writer?

JORDAN

To the craft born. This just pays the rent. Not that I don't enjoy talking with you.

CHRIS

Do you?

JORDAN

Do I what?

CHRIS

Enjoy talking with … people like me.

JORDAN

People like you? You mean writers in general? No. Some depressed writers are a real pain. They go on and on about how unfair the world is.

CHRIS

It is unfair.

JORDAN

Hello, I know that, but there's a difference between recognizing a fact and beating the life out of it.

CHRIS

Yes, that's true.

JORDAN

I try to ask them, "You think you're treated badly? Have you read the news in the last fifty years?" But it's a little like when your parents tell you to eat your food because there are starving children in Africa. You get it, right? But you're still dealing with a vegetable that makes you nauseous.

CHRIS

Or roast beef. That was mine. Yuck.

JORDAN

Right? That type never listens. Too sunk into themselves. It's like I'm not even here, like there's not another human being on the other end. There are days I want to kill myself. Hello! Human being here. Right?

CHRIS

Right.

JORDAN

So enough about you. I'm kidding.

CHRIS

I didn't mind you talking. I enjoyed hearing about the job.

JORDAN

That's why I said I enjoy talking to you. You're a good listener.

CHRIS

I am?

JORDAN

Yep. So let's get back to—

CHRIS

—Right, OK, yes.

JORDAN

Even though we don't have a self-defenestration package, we do have something for jumpers. We offer the Crane.

CHRIS

The Crane?

JORDAN

Yes, as in Mr. Hart Crane. He threw himself—

CHRIS

—Overboard from a ship.

JORDAN

You have done your research. Yes, so no risk to others. There's a lesson there for the hangers too. All too often they do it in a residence they share with a life partner. In their despair they forget about the impact on the person who finds them, swinging there in their own home. It's a horrifying spectacle, absolutely traumatizing.

CHRIS

I don't have a life partner to worry about.

JORDAN

I understand. I almost gave up on that proposition myself and then, poof! Out of the blue, who should enter my lonely terrestrial orbit than the partner of my dreams. These things happen, so never say never. In fact, I think that's why eighty percent of our customers are still alive and kicking today.

CHRIS

What? What do you mean?

JORDAN

When they receive our product, I think they feel … relieved. Somehow, having it makes them hold on a while long—

CHRIS

—I won't be holding on a while longer. I've held on too long already. I've got no one to worry about, and no one to worry about me, and I'm tired. I'm old before I'm old. I'm done.

JORDAN

I understand, and we're here to help. All we'll need from you is the writing submission for the final note. Once we have that and your choice of—

CHRIS

—I've already done the note. How soon can I submit it to you?

JORDAN

Immediately, if you're in a rush.

CHRIS

You mean, now?

JORDAN

Unless you have an unorthodox understanding of the word "immediately." Yes, now would be fine.

CHRIS

Great, should I—

JORDAN

—Email it to me directly. It's Jordan at exit strategies dot com.

CHRIS

J-o-r-d-a-n?

JORDAN

Right.

CHRIS

Case sensitive?

JORDAN

No.

CHRIS

Exit Strategies one word or with an underscore?

JORDAN

One word.

CHRIS

OK … there, sent.

JORDAN

OK … got it. Let me open, make sure everything is in order…

(pause)

CHRIS

Are you still there?
(pause)
Hello?

JORDAN

Wow.

CHRIS

What?

JORDAN

Wow, wow.

CHRIS

What are you—

JORDAN

—Wow, wow, wow.

CHRIS

I don't know what—

JORDAN

—You are an amazing writer.

Pause.

CHRIS

I am?

JORDAN

Extraordinary.

CHRIS

Are you playing with me?

JORDAN

Do I sound like someone who plays with the emotions of struggling artists? Let's pretend you didn't say that, shall we? Your writing is superb. If I may be so bold, I see traces of Proust, but without the excess, and a kind of Alice-Munro-ish understated-anguish. Now shall we complete your order?

CHRIS is frozen.

JORDAN

Are you there? … Hello? … Hellooo?

CHRIS goes to his desk, to his laptop, starts writing.
JORDAN ends the call and takes a new one.

JORDAN

Exit Strategies, Writer's Department, this is Jordan, may I help you?

Lights down. End of play.

The Age

BY BARRY CHARMAN

A man, the FIRST speaker, stands on a box at the centre of the stage. Two women, AGNES and ANNIE, stand over at the right of the stage, talking quietly amongst themselves.

Speaker #1: *(shouting)* The age of chivalry is dead!

ANNIE glances over to him

ANNIE : What did he say?

AGNES : He said the age of chivalry's dead.

ANNIE : No one stopped to tell me.

AGNES : He is telling you.

ANNIE : What, that was it?

AGNES : Yes.

ANNIE : There's no more?

AGNES : I don't think so.

ANNIE : Better go and ask him.

AGNES shrugs, then walks over to the FIRST speaker, who has not moved.

AGNES : Is that it?

SPEAKER #1 : It?

AGNES : I mean, well, what age is it then?

A SECOND man walks on stage with a second box. He puts his box down to the right of the FIRST Speaker, and stands on it.

SPEAKER #2 : *(loudly)* The age of chivalry is dead!

AGNES : We heard. What age is it now?

SPEAKER #2 : The age of artifice.

SPEAKER #1 : That's a lie!

SPEAKER #2 : Yes. The age of artifice has begun.

AGNES : *(to Speaker #1)* What did *you* think it was?

SPEAKER #1 : The age of bitterness.

AGNES : Bitterness?

SPEAKER #2 : *(mocking)* Oh, the age of truth!

AGNES : I'd rather have truth than lies.

SPEAKER #2 : Truth that leaves a bitter taste!

AGNES looks from one man to the other, then goes back to ANNIE.

ANNIE : Well?

AGNES : It's either the age of bitterness or artifice.

ANNIE : They can't decide?

AGNES : No.

ANNIE : It's not very *proper*, is it?

AGNES : No…

ANNIE : If there's a new age, we should know exactly what it's about.

AGNES : True.

ANNIE : How can we not know what age we live in? It wouldn't be *proper*.

AGNES : *(nodding)* Quite right.

A THIRD man walks on stage. He also has a box, and places it to the left of the FIRST man, then stands upon it.

SPEAKER #3 : The age of chivalry is dead!

AGNES : We know!

SPEAKER #3 : Oh.

Everyone now stares at the THIRD Speaker.

AGNES : Go on, what age is it, then?

SPEAKER #3 : The age of contrition.

SPEAKER #1 : Lies!

SPEAKER #2 : Which proves it's the age of artifice!

SPEAKER #1 : Exactly what a man might try and say in the age of bitterness!

SPEAKER #3 : *(frowning)* Artifice? Bitterness?

SPEAKER #1 : *(fervently)* Yes. *Truth. Despair. Regret.*

SPEAKER #2 : *(as fervently)* Lies! All revealing lies!

SPEAKER #3 : I don't know what you're talking about, either of you. The age of contrition has come.

SPEAKER #1 : Is this bitterness?

SPEAKER #2 : Are these lies?

SPEAKER #3 : *(firmly)* I will not be tricked.

SPEAKER #1 : Isn't this a bitter path?

SPEAKER #2 : Are you not simply resigned to the life of lies?

SPEAKER #3 : No.

SPEAKER #1 : Just fear?

SPEAKER #2 : Just abasement?

SPEAKER #3 : I never mentioned these things.

SPEAKER #2 : But there must be contrition?

SPEAKER #1 : Before our judges?

SPEAKER #3 : Before our betters. Now is the time people should prostrate themselves before worthier men. Their saviours, who have set a path for them to follow.

SPEAKER #2 : *(mocking)* A theory spun out of lies!

SPEAKER #1 : *(mocking)* A fantasy born of bitterness!

SPEAKER #3 : *(emotionally)* No! You both are frauds, who need to conform, who need to be controlled, proving the age of contrition is now!

The three speakers fall silent, glaring at each other. After a moment all three look to AGNES and ANNIE.

SPEAKER #2 : What age?

AGNES : You're asking us?

SPEAKER #1 : *(tensely)* Perhaps.

SPEAKER #3 : Let the people decide. Let them recognise us.

AGNES : Why did the age of chivalry die?

SPEAKER #3 : Because it was rejected.

SPEAKER #1 : Mortal.

SPEAKER #2 : Ruined.

ANNIE : Ruined?

SPEAKER #2 : *(deliberately)* By cynical women.

ANNIE and AGNES exchange shocked looks.

ANNIE : Did you hear that?

AGNES : I did.

ANNIE : That's putting the blame right on my doorstep, that is.

AGNES : *(sneering)* They're just cynical men.

ANNIE : Did they respect the age of chivalry?

AGNES : Good question- did they?

They look at the three men, who look uncertain.

SPEAKER #1 : Sad to think, but it doesn't matter anymore.

SPEAKER #2 : Yes.

SPEAKER #3 : That age is dead.

SPEAKER #1 : Buried in bitterness.

SPEAKER #2 : Consumed by lies.

SPEAKER #3 : Desperate for redemption.

The three speakers glare at each other. ANNIE and AGNES look to each other, trying to ignore the men.

ANNIE : What was before the age of chivalry?

AGNES : I don't know...

ANNIE : It could've come round again.

AGNES considers, then shakes her head.

AGNES : Don't think they do, dear, don't think they do.

ANNIE : Oh.

AGNES : But what *did* come before?

ANNIE : Was it the age of reason?

AGNES : The age of reason?

AGNES laughs. She looks over to the three speakers, who look impatient.

She thinks there was an age of reason!

The speakers alternately laugh and shake their heads. Their mood improves briefly.

SPEAKER #3 : *(muttered)* An age of reason… You wouldn't know what you were getting.

AGNES turns back to ANNIE.

AGNES : I don't think we had an age of reason.

ANNIE : What was I thinking of, then?

AGNES : I'm sure I don't know, love.

ANNIE : Something *reasonable* perhaps, that wasn't actually an age of reason?

SPEAKER #1 : Oh good grief.

AGNES glances back at him.

AGNES : I'm sure the age of chivalry is still in effect for a while, so why don't you button it and let her think!

AGNES turns back to ANNIE. The FIRST speaker glances at the THIRD.

SPEAKER #1 : Is it?

SPEAKER #3 : What?

SPEAKER #1 : Still the age of chivalry?

SPEAKER #3 : *(defensively)* Are you suggesting I don't know an age of chivalry when I live in it. I am offended.

SPEAKER #2 : *(quietly)* Ignorance suggests an age has passed.

They look back to ANNIE and AGNES, who are lost in thought.

ANNIE : It was the age of appetite.

AGNES : *(sneering)* Oh yes. The age of perfidy and pampering. Expenditure. Excellence.

ANNIE : Trivial men made trinkets for trivial men.

AGNES : Out of air.

ANNIE : There was no money. Where was the money?

AGNES : There was no money.

They nod at each other.

You remember it?

ANNIE : I remember a hollow stomach. A sunken face on a child. A parade of ribs.

AGNES : They tried to make it the age of opportunity. Then the age of maturity-

ANNIE : All failed.

AGNES : All the sum of the other.

ANNIE : It hasn't come round again.

AGNES : *(distantly)* I don't think that they do… Or is that all they do?

They stare at each other, troubled. The three men are looking more impatient.

SPEAKER #1 : *(to Speaker #3)* Don't you feel at all broken? Betrayed? Bitter?

SPEAKER #3 : No. I am humbled. Contrite.

SPEAKER #2 : Humbled? By who?

SPEAKER #3 : By those with the wisdom to give me a second chance. It is *wisdom* that contrition brings.

SPEAKER #2 : Then why not call it the age of wisdom?

SPEAKER #3 : People wilfully misinterpret wisdom.

SPEAKER #1 : They do?

SPEAKER #3 : Yes. The poor man thinks he can rise above himself, he grasps at an illusion and becomes a mockery. The wealthy man relaxes, and gives his inferiors freedom, he expects them to reward him, but what they taste drives them to delirium.

Pause.

(quietly) Expectations must be limited. Narrowed. The age must be precise.

ANNIE and AGNES have been conferring, now they look back at the three men.

AGNES : We've decided.

SPEAKER #1 : Oh?

ANNIE : Yes, it is the age of doubt.

SPEAKER #2 : I doubt that.

ANNIE : See?

SPEAKER #2 : Ah, but I was lying, and so were you.

ANNIE : *(startled)* No, I wasn't.

SPEAKER #2 : You wouldn't even be aware of it. It comes naturally now.

SPEAKER #1 : *(to Annie)* You only called it the age of doubt, because you were bitter, right?

SPEAKER #3 : Bitterly in need of contrition.

AGNES : You said we could decide!

SPEAKER #1: You haven't been clear enough.

SPEAKER #3 : We're all doubtful about different things.

ANNIE : So?

SPEAKER #3 : There should be only one doubt.

ANNIE : That doesn't make any sense.

SPEAKER #2 : The age of doubt is based on lies.

SPEAKER #1 : Words slipped through the bars of bitter teeth!

AGNES : *(shouting)* Stop it! Stop it! Why do we *have* to choose?

ANNIE : Yes, why?

SPEAKER #1 : You have to choose.

SPEAKER #2 : You have to choose one of us.

SPEAKER #3 : You have three choices. That is the system.

AGNES : We can't *not* choose?

SPEAKER #1 : *(appalled)* Not choose?!

SPEAKER #2 : Everyone must choose!

SPEAKER #3 : It's the choice that makes you free.

SPEAKER #1 : This is your way of accepting what comes.

SPEAKER #2 : What do *you* want?

SPEAKER #3 : The choices are *for* you.

ANNIE : But- but why does the age of chivalry *have* to end?

SPEAKER #1 : Cycles.

SPEAKER #2 : Yes, everything goes in cycles.

SPEAKER #3 : Every beginning is some other beginning's end.

SPEAKER #1 : And everything *must* end.

ANNIE : *(quietly)* But we don't want it to end.

The three speakers stare down at them impassively.

SPEAKER #1 : It is the age of bitterness.

SPEAKER #2 : The age of artifice.

SPEAKER #3 : The age of contrition.

SPEAKER #1 : Which?

AGNES : All. The age of doubt.

SPEAKER #2 : *(angrily)* You can't have them all.

ANNIE : But aren't you all of the same mind? Aren't you all but brothers?

The three men glance uneasily at each other.

SPEAKER #1 : We are unconnected.

SPEAKER #2 : Fierce rivals.

SPEAKER #3 : Nothing in common.

AGNES : Nothing but doubt?

SPEAKER #3 : Nothing at all.

ANNIE and AGNES look helplessly at each other.

ANNIE : Bitterness?

AGNES : A cynical word for acceptance. Don't think I want that.

ANNIE : Artifice?

AGNES : A trick- not even a lie- something worse.

ANNIE : Contrition?

Pause.

AGNES : Made to feel I've lived my life wrong? Made to feel small? There are worse things.

AGNES and ANNIE turn to the three men.

It's the age of contrition.

SPEAKER #3 : *(nodding)* Good. Good.

The THIRD speaker looks humble and gracious, the other speakers nod at him, and he nods back. The FIRST and SECOND speakers step down from their boxes, pick them up, and then move to the right of the stage, where they stand and wait.

ANNIE : *(to Speaker #3)* What happens now?

SPEAKER #3 : What? Oh, an age of humility, of penitence and new understanding. A time of earning the trust and love of your betters. A time to bow.

AGNES : Will you bow with us?

SPEAKER #3 : Of course, I will be there in spirit.

ANNIE : And where in fact?

SPEAKER #3 : Wherever this age sees fit to put me.

He smiles at them, then steps down, takes his box, and goes over to the other two speakers. They all talk quietly amongst themselves.

AGNES : *(awkwardly)* Well, I'm glad we got to choose.

ANNIE : Yes. I'm glad we were given a choice.

AGNES : It'll be *good* to look back and know we had a choice.

They study each other, both a little uncertain. After a moment, they smile falteringly, then walk off stage, arm in arm.

When they are gone, the three speakers, huddled in the corner, laugh and pat each other on the back. The lights dim.

The End.

Burst

BY JAYNE MAREK

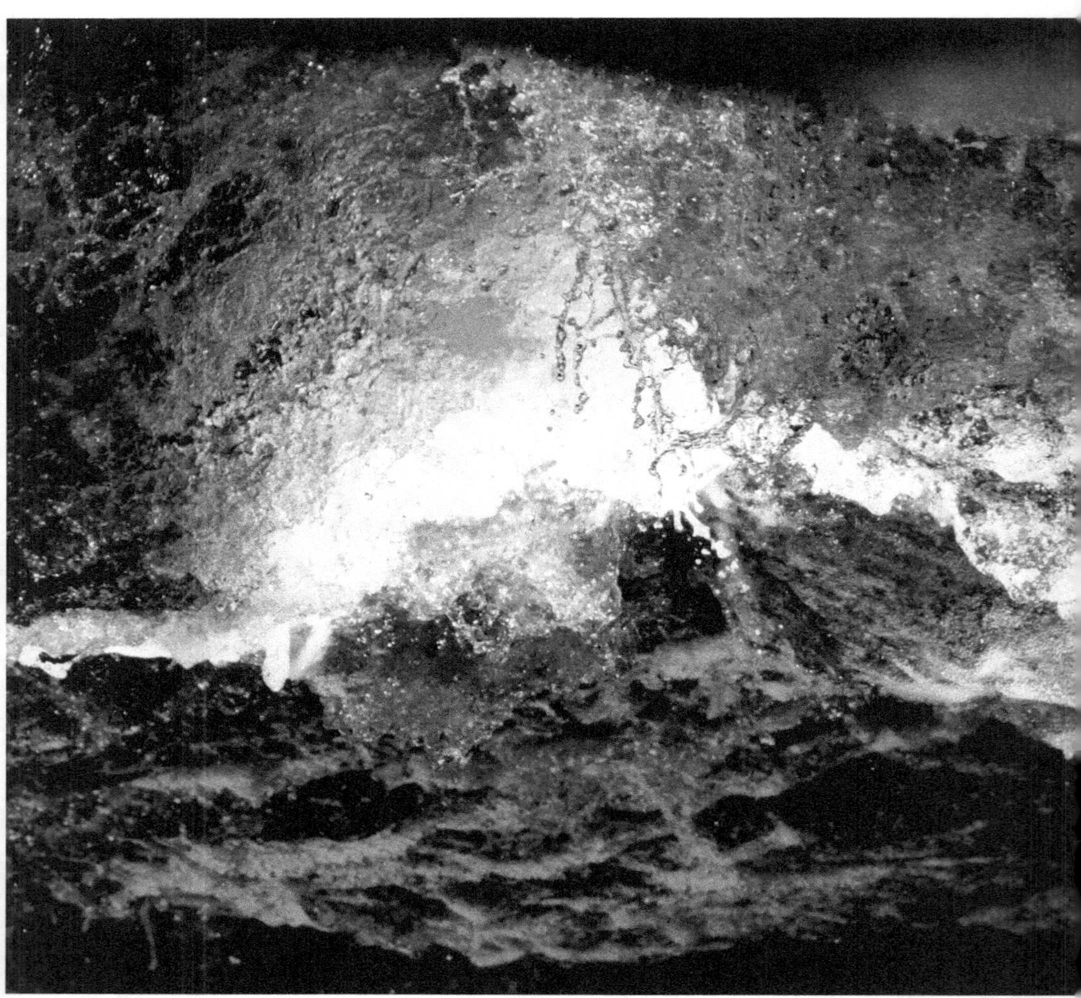

DIGITAL PHOTOGRAPH, 3857px x 2578px, 2016

Ecce homo

BY NELLY SANCHEZ

Geneva

BY KANDRA LYN SCULLIN

INTAGLIO ETCHING/AQUATINT, 4in x 6in 2017

Le cheval damour

BY NELLY SANCHEZ

COLLAGE, 30cm x 40cm, 2017

Octopus

BY ZACHARY BOWMAN

"Octopus" is part of "Aquasition" which is a series contemporary oil paintings on primed wooden boards (16x20inches) all of them have been made since the start of 2018.

Ode to the Mundane

BY ANA BROTAS

PHOTOGRAM ANALOGUE TECHNIQUE, 15cm x 20cm, 2017

Just Let Go

BY RACHEL D.

DIGITAL, 7.66in x 10.443in, 2016

Eve ou la connaissance

BY NELLY SANCHEZ

COLLAGE, 40cm x 35cm, 2016

Winter Solstice

BY GABRIELLE LANGLEY

There is a silence that circles itself
while we sleep.
I have learned to keep my secrets
in the silver veins of ice-white marble.
I have learned to count my sins
on an abacus strung with pearls.

Beneath this snow, there are vines.
The roots weave through skeletons
wrap themselves around ankle and wrist bones.
They make me remember other nights.

I am deaf
but I still hear your footsteps.
I am mute
but I still repeat your name.
The petals of strange flowers
sing in my mouth.

Perhaps in the spring
sparrows will learn to sing
in the blistered throats of bell towers.
In the summer
we may pour ourselves out

like pale blue sand
on a cypress peer
like a sky robbed of its rain.
In the fall a wind of monarchs
might escape from a wall of fire.

Until then, I wait in this place
where madonnas and martyrs
weep among their lilies
where the scent of faded orange blossom
is still trying to rise from the whispers
of broken families.

I remember that my own remains
are buried here, with a lost bridal veil, buried
beneath a trellis that warmer weather will dress
in star jasmine and honeysuckle.

The stars rise and strike at midnight
like countless darts.
The moon spills her light
like salt in a wound.
The air has turned cold.

Perhaps the children
standing here above my grave
will learn how to keep warm
nestling deep into the fur
of white animals.
Perhaps they will celebrate
Christmas.

But when all of their churches finally fall
when all of their cities have burned
you will find this poem, left for you
like a flower hidden in the ashes.

Haunted by Ancestors

BY GS MURPHY

every day I wake with the ashes of my ancestors,
smudged on my chest
echoed drum beats of the seven clans communing with sky-father,
earth-mother and the four directions of the sacred.

each step in this modern world is a reminder of conquest,
genocide, broken treatise and stories stolen,
a culture that hails Columbus, conquistadors, pilgrims and sadist,

insults in passing parking meters,
'for-rent' signs, dream catchers dangling off rear-view mirrors, yet
no-one looks back,

insults in 'wild-indians', 'off the reservation', Kansas –city
chiefs, Cleveland braves, Washington redskins, the only red-skin I
recognize is potatoes,

our chiefs are dead, only elders remain and they soon will die,
medicine has a new meaning, the infusion of culture, religion and
respect dissipate with morning dew,

I exist in salaried wages,
suit and tie necessity, hunting in grocery aisles on land better fit
for gathering freely

there is no politics for the dead, the endangered species known as
indigenous, we've even lost our skin-tone, big-noses, silent rage
and native solace are all that remains,

there was poetry in the daily quest,
the inter-dependent nature of our people,
there was love in the mud,
there was nobility in the first mobile homes made of wood and
skin now shelter bought with our time.

time that's run out, reflection that comes as stereotypes, it was
our turn to listen to things that will speak in language that died
centuries ago,
now drowned by technology and noise pollution,

my skin is white, my blood is red,
my spirit is cha-la-gee,
my spirit is Equa Nvyu
my heart is in the earth with ancestors,
in my hands are the offerings of tobacco and reverence

each night is lit with sage, sweet grass and smudge,
I fall sleep to drum-beats in my chest,
and burn campfires in my dreams only to wake in the morning
with ashes over my heart.

Blackbody Radiation

BY LAURA LILLY

– after The Orphan Master's Son by Adam Johnson

Shrimp came in swarms
the night we hauled
tennis shoes up in the nets –
mismatched red left and blue
right, silver Nike swooshes
on salt-scrubbed canvas.
The Second Mate threw his
rubber boots overboard,
lacing on a pair of women's trainers.
"These are all the rage in the Capital."

"How would you know?
You've never been."

The shrimp pulsed translucently,
kicking through the air, glowing
like light-up children's sneakers.

The next evening, we set longlines
for sharks, winching their torpid bodies
onboard to carve five quick slices

before slipping them back over the side
to spiral helplessly down - no fins
left to resist gravity's tug.

Afterward, I pointed the radio overhead
to capture the Americans and Russians
playing chess in space, their pieces

drifting weightlessly out of reach.
Between us, the night sky
sprinkled itself

above the horizon, stars
as flashing pinpricks swirling
endlessly overhead.

Guide to Loneliness

BY JOSEPHINE SIMPSON

When this feeling comes, don't fight it.
Let the iron weight attached to your diaphragm sink
through the ocean of your intestines.
Don't fear that it might pull you under—
let it drag you down to the dark peace of the benthic zone.

Cross-legged and still,
feel the millennia-slow current
slide by.
Let it touch you the way you have been longing to be touched on
these
millennia-long nights.

The lights of the angler fish
can be gazed upon similarly to the night sky,
but know that they are closer,
almost close enough to touch,
and they are breathing.
Match your breath to theirs.
They know the steady pace of survival in the depths.

Eventually, you will rise, bloated, to the surface.

The Sleepers

BY SIDDHARTH KATRAGADDA

sprawled across two seats on the subway,
a man that was as dead as clay;
if you watered him a bit
he would even sprout beefsteak tomatoes all day

and a few sunflowers too; people walked by,
buried in their phones; stations came and went all day,
and at night, on my way back,
find him still in his partial state of decay;

a big bag of living human cells holding
an extra-large coke and a discarded parfait;
he could be god, for all you know,
watching us in disguise, on his brief stay.

A Geobiography

BY JEFFERY KNAPP

I grew up and came of age among loblolly pines
In languorous red clay landscapes,
Where the Piedmont sinks into the Black Belt
And the fall line dissipates like a lazy ellipsis...
Springtime was a kaleidoscope of blooms,
Azalea and camellia, mimosa and wisteria.
Along hedgerows like hummingbirds
We snacked upon honeysuckle nectar.
Through the long, drowsy, seemingly endless summer,
Plump tomatoes and thick-skinned muscadines
Recompensed us for hot, sticky days and humid nights.
A mature magnolia rose in the backyard
From roots knobby like grandma's veins,
A high refuge for a clambering boy's escape,
Its crown wavering lofty and free.
I left at twenty-five, yet still today when
I drive the causeway across the Chattahoochee
And see Eufaula's bluffs loom ahead,
I know I can't elude the hold Alabama has on me.

I made my life and begot my progeny
Among live oaks, Spanish moss, and alien palms,
Where salt marshes insist their way inland
And shade is precious.
My home is red hills, cold springs, and lowlands
Once covered by shallow Cretaceous seas.
The pathways of my adulthood amble
From St. Andrews Bay to the Matanzas
Along trails trodden by Apalachee and Timucua,
Then carved by Spaniards to make a road
Six horses wide, christened the
Camino Real.
Here we hunker down for hurricanes
With deceptive nonchalance, natural
As a belly full of shrimp and oysters.
When I return from abroad,
The scents of north Florida,
Dank, faintly rotting, tinged with salt spray,
Welcome me fondly, and easy
I breathe the thick familiar air.

But my bones were formed from stony ground,
From slate and red shale, where
Haudenosaunee men and women
Knapped flint to hunt game beside
The Mohawk, where Englishmen and French
Clashed along a shifting frontier.
My people felled timber, milked Holsteins,
And dug the Erie Canal, to twine with
Her sister river and carry the load
For settlers heading west, until
Iron rails took up her burden and
Left her lying a useless ditch.
On a rare pilgrimage, the first in fifteen years,
The second in twenty-five,
I was unprepared for the feelings
My native home birthed in me.

How could I know that this land,
These hillocks, these fields of corn,
These abandoned barns, unpainted, hollow,
These decaying towns with their
Bricks crumbling and roofs collapsing,
Would draw me like a lodestone
To feel deep in my marrow
The atavistic pull of generations.
Who dwelt here, lived and died here?
How could I have known?
And what do I do with this,
This ligature that's tied off with me?
My children don't know this place,
Don't love this place,
Nor will they.
That bond has been broken.

Sōma sēma, the body is a tomb.
So said the Greeks, but why should we mourn?
A casket filled with Carpathian soil
Was not Vlad's prison, but rather
His sanctuary, his stronghold,
And he lived five hundred years.
Yet sēma also means an omen, a portent,
A sign sent from the gods.

Our bodies respond to place, a signal to our souls,
As certain places seek to commune,
Though somehow we missed the message.
Perhaps this hovering revelation
Which fails to materialize
Is the aesthetic moment,
The razor's edge that beauty walks.
Perhaps our yearning for fulfillment,
Our need to weave a web of sense,
Has driven us from the places
That conjured our bones from dust
Since the first mortals stood erect
And scanned the African savanna,
Searching for hints of a new home,
As the gods beckoned them onward
And scattered them across the earth.

Ode to Coffee

BY PATRICIA O'BRIEN

To wake in the quiet morning
wood floor cool against bare feet
summoned to the kitchen
to the coffee maker
that sits like a huddled monk
measuring grounds with a silver scoop
to brew a perfect cup of joe
in a porcelain cup
dark and delicious
inhaling aromatherapy
elixir of well-being
from South America's highlands
deep notes of bitter roast
with a touch of cream.
To sip is bliss
as wakefulness creeps in
with the daylight
that dispels night's shadows
and its residue of dreams.
The glory of the ordinary
cup of strength, cup of light, cup of song
to keep the mind and sky open
in this slow moving hour
when all is possible
before being swallowed
by the rush of the world.

The First Night Without You

BY JORDAN NISHKIAN

means resting on pillows
          in the shape of a hangman
          who guessed a letter too many,
an echoing bloodstream
          feigning beats
          of a secondary life,
scratches at 400-count linens
          to pick up scents that
          you left behind in the fabric,
relearning to take up
          the expanse of mattress where
          coils remember the weight of your limbs.

Take Note

BY STUART GUNTER

Certainly, nothing is this simple.
After the war, the people hung
Mussolini upside down from steel
girders in the Piazzale Loreto,
where they beat him with their fists,
shot him, and hit him with stones
and hammers. This is what we do:
we build up our idols only to destroy
them in the end.

When We Fight

BY JASON FORBACH

When we fight
we hit hard
and fast.
The force of gravity.
A dropped glass
on the kitchen floor
that sends shrapnel in every direction,
silvery shards,
a dangerous spray.
So we step away
from the point of impact,
sweep up the scattered
pieces
and replace a new
tumbler
on the shelf
next to the others.

How beautiful they all look
untouched there
in rows,
awaiting their turn.

Some days later
I'm sure to find
eagerly awaiting
on the floor,
winking
under the sink
or by the refrigerator,
a forgotten shiv
with the softest
most delicate part
of the bottom of my
bare foot.
Remnants certain
to draw bloody
footsteps,

shards of
serrated words
certain to sink deep
into my flesh,
certain to scar,
a familiar razor
reminding me of
our broken pieces
that I had vowed never to step on,
ever again.

But we are
always,
always,
always
dropping
Glasses.

Doubt Is Not Our Birthright

BY KERRI LADISH

For years I taught myself how to flail,
falter, hesitate, waiver, a precursor
for eventually failing—which always
looked a lot like never beginning.

I excelled at drowning
in what-ifs, could and should
and maybe someday would-bes,
too content to sit in this half-light,
tongue-twisted and tied up for a half-life.

I spent so much time suppressing
passion ability clarity wisdom, burying it
instead of listening to my blood that is her blood
that is their blood—that is the blood of a thousand wombs:
magic and potent

visceral and always breathing. Blood that cries out
when everything else
goes quiet.

Blood that charts a course
even as we try so desperately
to fill every moment with movement,
sound, plans, activities, ever more proclivities.

We spend so much time quieting voices
with as much right to scream
sing praise astonish.

Listen
Listen
Listen

We've been trying to tell you:

You have nothing left
to lose.

Dialogue with a Space Cadet

BY MATTHEW MAPES

who could love another planet
as their home after earth
we leave like vikings, dead and
burning at the same time
hungry for rocks and gravity
an ocean, anything that sinks

anyway, the rocket's full
I'm not leaving, the earth is
dropping out of the race soon
I'll sit here like a sentry
waiting for an old king's ghost
something for my mother's heart

I remember when she sang
for me, to sleep, windy hands
fidgeting with my hair
I'm gonna wait for the bubble
to pop, the last solar wind to blow
and all the grass to die

it's not romantic to stay in love
when you're young,
heavenly vessel capsizing in a way
that makes god blush
but who could love another planet
space is a dial tone

Dear Reader

BY ADAM TAVEL

For all I know, you hate the squeak of shoes
across your kitchen tile, the nervous way
I clear my throat when conversations turn
to wine, or just the sight of ponytails
on men whose temples gray. I have no clue
what you can't forgive. Your window frames
a different smidge of earth. Sometimes I yearn
to sing the birthday song into a wail
but mime my tuneless lips instead. Silence
makes a melody of awkward air
that later blows the candles out. My gift
is a small token wrapped hysterically
with the obituary page. If you sift
you'll find the one who clutched at sirens.

Biographies

Prose

RACHEL BROWNING

Rachel Browning is an attorney, writer, and musician originally from Houston, Texas. Her short fiction has appeared in *Every Day Fiction*, *The Write Launch*, and *The Esthetic Apostle*. She currently lives in Maryland with her wife and twin daughters.

TYLER CORBRIDGE

Tyler Corbridge lives in Tuscaloosa. He is a husband, recent father, and former milkman. His work has appeared or will soon appear in *Salt Hill Journal*, *Chicago Quarterly Review*, *Gravel: A Literary Journal*, *Five Quarterly*, and *Elsewhere Magazine*, among others. He is currently a creative writing instructor and MFA candidate at the University of Alabama, though he sometimes wishes he were still driving his milk truck in the Wasatch Mountains of Utah.

ILZE B. DUARTE

Ilze B. Duarte writes short prose and translates works by contemporary Brazilian writers. Her translations appear or are forthcoming in *Your Impossible Voice* and *The Massachusetts Review*. Ms. Duarte lives with her husband and two daughters in Milpitas, California.

CATIE PRENDERGAST

Catie Prendergast is a writer and editor from New York City currently residing in Los Angeles. Her creative non-fiction has appeared online in *The New York Times Magazine*, *Modern Farmer*, *Thought Catalog*, and *Elite Daily*, and her poetry has appeared on *Internet Poetry*.

ETHAN WARREN

Ethan Warren is a staff writer for the film journal *Bright Wall/ Dark Room*. He is also the director of the award-winning indie feature film *West of Her*, and the recipient of the Boston Project Playwriting Fellowship from SpeakEasy stage company. A graduate of the MFA program at the University of North Carolina Wilmington, his writing has been featured in *New Limestone*

Review, *Furious Gazelle*, and *Stage-It! 10-minute Plays*. He lives in the Boston area with his wife, Caitlin, and their daughter, Nora.

Plays

BARRY CHARMAN

barrycharman.blogspot.co.uk

Barry Charman is a writer living in North London. He has been published in various magazines, including *Ambit*, *Firewords Quarterly*, *Bare Fiction Magazine*, and *Popshot*. He has had poems published online and in print, most recently in *Bewildering Stories* and *The Linnet's Wings*.

ANDREW R. HEINZE

Andrew R. Heinze is the award-winning author of *Jews and the American Soul*. His full-length plays include *Deleting Dad*, winner of Texas Nonprofit Theatres' 2016 New Play competition, and *The Inventions of the Living Room*, winner Texas NonProfit Theatres' 2014 New Play competition, among many others. Andrew's one-act plays have been produced in New York, Los Angeles, Seattle, Austin, Denver, Albuquerque, and elsewhere. They include the award-winning comedies *The FQ* (about obscenity, cable TV) and *The Bar Mitzvah of Jesus Goldfarb,* and the award-winning drama *Masha: Conditions in the Holy Land.*

Visual Art

ZACHARY BOWMAN

Zach Bowman's life has been saturated with the world of art. It was natural for him to develop an affinity for art, as he watched his mother teach hundreds of students, creating magic within the walls of her studio. Zach's work has much to do with his love of life, humanity, and light. As he paints in oil, he aims to reflect the depth and radiance of each person, as well as the natural luminous environments that surround them. Each layer of oil paint catches light in its own way and reveals the true beauty of each person to the viewer through the interaction of the passing layers with true jewel colors that lay deep within

ANA BROTAS

Ana Brotas is a Portuguese multidisciplinary artist interested in material and aesthetic manipulation in order to tell stories. The constant search to find appropriate forms of visual storytelling has led her to explore a wide range of mediums, consistently embracing a playful discourse that connects art with her social and ecological contexts. She studied Cinema at the Film and Theater School of Lisbon and Fine Art at both Central Saint Martins and Goldsmiths University of London. Her work has been exhibited and published internationally. She was awarded at Camberwell's and Deptford's Contemporary Visual Arts Festivals. Her latest commissions include a public interactive billboard for WeTransfer and an interactive performance piece for the Sydney Opera House. Currently, she is coordinating the MAE arts project.

RACHEL D.

patreon.com/AsteroidBelt
asteroidbeltstudio.bandcamp.com

Rachel D. makes songs, zines, comics, and poems, but she also enjoys writing prose.

JAYNE MAREK

Jayne Marek has provided color cover art for *Silk Road*, *Bombay Gin*, *The Bend*, and for her two full-length poetry books, *In and Out of Rough Water* and *The Tree Surgeon Dreams of Bowling*. Her poetry and art photos appear in *Grub Street*, *The Cortland Review*, *Lunch Ticket*, *The Lake*, *Raven Chronicles*, *Stonecoast Review*, *Women's Studies Quarterly*, *Gulf Stream*, *Amsterdam Quarterly*, *About Place Journal*, *Notre Dame Review*, and elsewhere. She has received two Pushcart Prize nominations.

NELLY SANCHEZ

nellysanchez.fr

Nelly Sanchez is a French *collagiste*, inspired by surrealism and futurism. Her universe is a feminine one, sensual, coloured, mysterious, sometimes funny, often disturbing. Her artworks are like mirrors, full of symbols. Her main themes are the woman's condition and relationships between men and women. Her collages serve as a compliment to her writings on a novel about French women.

KANDRA LYN SCULLIN

kandrascullin.myportfolio.com

Kandra Scullin is a full-time artist living in Calimesa, California. She works as a part-time art professor for California State University San Bernardino. In addition to teaching, three of her most valued roles in life are being a mother, wife, and friend.

Poetry

JASON FORBACH

Jason Forbach is an actor and writer from New York City. His play *Heathen Hill* placed in the New Works of Merit Playwriting Competition.

STUART GUNTER

Stuart Gunter lives in Schuyler, Virginia, with his wife and two children, two dogs, and two cats. He likes to paddle the Rockfish River and play drums in obscure rock bands. His poetry has appeared in *Whurk*, *The Sow's Ear Poetry Review*, *Waxing & Waning*, and *The Artemis Journal*, among others.

SIDDHARTH KATRAGADDA

Sid Katragadda is the author of two novels in verse, *Dark Rooms* and *The Other Wife*, which won the San Diego Book Awards. He has also written an unpublished novel. His work has been published on CNN and other reputed journals. He's also an award-winning screenwriter and artist. He lives in San Diego, California.

JEFFERY KNAPP

Jeffery Knapp has recently started writing poetry again after a long absence. Most recently Jeffery's poem "477" was included in the anthology *Howl, 2016! Poems, Rants, and Essays on the Election.*

KERRI LADISH

Twitter: @kerrianne

Instagram: @kerri_anne

Kerri Anne Ladish is a northwest native, storyteller, and mountain dweller. Words of hers have been published or are forthcoming in *Hedgehog Poetry*, *THIS Literary Magazine*, *Kindling*, *Keep It Wild*, *Drabble Rousers*, and *Fortunates*.

GABRIELLE LANGLEY

gabriellelangley.com

Gabrielle Langley has been featured in *Huffington Post* as one of Houston's important emerging poets. She is a recipient of the Lorene Pouncey Award and Houston Poetry Fest's Jury Prize. She is also a co-founder and editor of *Red Sky: Poetry on the Global Epidemic of Violence Against Women.* Her debut collection of poetry, "Azaleas on Fire," will be released in early 2019.

LAURA LILLY

Laura Lilly is an oceanographer, sailor, and surfer whose poetic interests encompass ships at sea, the intricacies of wave formation, and life in Baja California, all with the common theme of examining minute human interactions. She is based in San Diego, California, where she engages with all of the above plus horse polo and occasional trips to the mountains.

MATTHEW MAPES

Matthew Mapes is a poet living and writing in Houston, Texas, after graduating from Eastern Washington University's MFA program in Spokane, Washington.

GS MURPHY

GS Murphy is a poet and photographer currently living in Geneva, New York. Murphy often writes from a personal, intimate perspective with themes such as family life, motorcycles, firefighting, spirituality, and some nonsensical subjects. He lives with his wife and two very spoiled dogs.

JORDAN NISHKIAN

Born and raised near the Pacific Coast, Jordan Nishkian is a California girl through and through. For as long as she can remember, she's always had a passion for the expression of art and has explored nearly every form she could get her hands on. Although she has had a career in the performing arts, writing will always be her home base. After graduating from Cal State Long Beach with a BA in Creative Writing and a BA in Anthropology, she has gone on to write for a handful of publications, businesses, and websites. While she hopes to one day be found on the editor's page of a magazine, for now you can find her curled up in a comfy chair with a book in her hand and a pen in her hair.

PATRICIA O'BRIEN

Patricia O'Brien grew up in Newtown Square, Pennsylvania. She received a BA in English Literature and a minor in teaching from Saint Joseph's University, and an MA in Contemporary British and American Literature from West Chester University. O'Brien's poems have appeared in *The English Journal*, *Mad Poets Review*, *Schuylkill Valley Journal of the Arts*, and *Philadelphia Poets* to name a few. She published a chapbook entitled *Catching Fire* in 2016. O'Brien taught literature at Villa Maria Academy and creative writing at Penn State Brandywine. Currently, she works in patient management. She and her husband live in West Chester, Pennsylvania and have two daughters.

JOSEPHINE SIMPSON

Josephine Simpson is an emerging writer from Cortes Island, British Columbia, where the gray, rainswept winters, and fruit-laden summers inspire her poems about simplicity, care, and longing.

ADAM TAVEL

adamtavel.com

Adam Tavel's third poetry collection, *Catafalque*, recently won the 2017 Richard Wilbur Book Award and is forthcoming with the University of Evansville Press. He is also the author of *The Fawn Abyss* and *Plash & Levitation*, winner of the Permafrost Book Prize in Poetry. His recent poems appear, or will soon appear, in *Verse Daily*, *Willow Springs*, *Crazyhorse*, *Copper Nickel*, *Pleiades*, *Third Coast*, *Atlanta Review*, and *Arts & Letters*, among others.

SUBMISSION INFORMATION

New Plains Review accepts original work in poetry, prose, and visual art. Submission information and editorial guidelines are accessible through the website, newplainsreview.com.

ORDERING INFORMATION

Pricing for current and back issues are available through Amazon.

www.ingramcontent.com/pod-product-compliance
Lightning Source LLC
Chambersburg PA
CBHW071010120726
47910CB00004B/1454

* 9 7 8 0 9 9 8 4 0 6 1 3 8 *